"ALGORITHMIC TRADING: Strategies, Technologies, and Tools for the Modern Market"

INDEX

Content

Gratitude 5

Prologue 6

Introduction 8

CHAPTER 1 10

1. Introduction to Algorithmic Trading 10

CHAPTER 2 19

Fundamentals of the Financial Market 19

CHAPTER 3 44

Algorithmic Trading Strategies 44

CHAPTER 4 65

Design and Development of Algorithms 65

CHAPTER 5 98

5. Data Analysis and Machine Learning in Trading 98

CHAPTER 6 106

Evaluation and Optimization of Strategies ... 106

CHAPTER 7 114

Implementation and Execution 114

CHAPTER 8 122

Legal and Regulatory Aspects 122

CHAPTER 9 128

Tools and Resources: Popular Algorithmic Trading Platforms 128

CHAPTER 10 141

ALGORITHMIC TRADING PROGRAMMING BUILDER 141

CHAPTER 11 150

VPS FOR HOSTING AND CONTINUOUS OPERATION 150

CHAPTER 12 160

Future Perspectives 160

ANNEXES 165

You can purchase this book at the following Amazon link : 212

Gratitude

I want to express my sincere gratitude for purchasing this book. Your interest in learning and improving your knowledge of **algorithmic trading** is an important step toward success in the financial markets. My goal with this book was to provide you with useful tools, practical strategies, and a clear understanding of this exciting form of trading.

I hope what you've learned here inspires you and helps you improve your trading skills. Remember that knowledge is the greatest asset on this path, and that constant practice and careful analysis are key to achieving your goals.

Prologue

The financial world has undergone an unprecedented transformation in recent decades, driven by the fusion of technology and global markets. This book, "Algorithmic Trading: Platforms, Languages, Builders, and VPS," emerges as an essential guide for those who wish to understand and master one of the most revolutionary areas of modern trading.

Algorithmic trading, a discipline that combines programming, financial analysis, and strategic execution, has not only democratized access to markets but has also redefined the way real-time decisions are made. From its origins in the 1970s, when computers began calculating theoretical prices, to its evolution into today's sophisticated high-frequency algorithms, this approach has proven to be a powerful tool for both retail and institutional traders.

This book is not just a technical manual; it's an invitation to delve into the fascinating world of automated trading. Here, readers will find not only clear explanations of fundamental concepts such as trading platforms, programming languages, and VPS servers, but also practical tools for developing their own strategies and executing them effectively.

As you progress through its pages, you'll discover how to choose the platform that best suits your needs, how to program strategies in languages like Python or MQL5, and how to ensure your algorithms operate uninterruptedly thanks to VPS servers. We'll also explore the creativity behind programming builders, which make algorithmic trading accessible even to those without advanced programming knowledge.

"Algorithmic Trading: Platforms, Languages, Builders, and VPS" is more than a book; it's a roadmap to the future of finance. My hope is that this work will inspire its readers to adopt an innovative mindset, to experiment fearlessly, and to leverage technological tools to achieve their goals in the markets.

Algorithmic trading isn't a privilege for the few; it's an opportunity available to all those willing to learn, adapt, and evolve.

Welcome to this exciting journey!

Introduction

The rapid advancement of technology has transformed every aspect of our lives, and the financial world has been no exception. Among the most significant innovations of recent decades is algorithmic trading, a discipline that merges programming and financial strategy to automate decisions and operations in global markets. This book, "Algorithmic Trading: Platforms, Languages, Builders, and VPS," aims to demystify this exciting field and provide a practical and accessible guide for traders of all levels.

Since its emergence in the 1970s, algorithmic trading has evolved from simple computerized calculations to sophisticated high-frequency systems capable of executing thousands of trades in milliseconds. This shift has not only democratized access to advanced investment tools but has also redefined the rules of the game in financial markets. Now, any trader with access to a computer, a stable internet connection, and basic programming skills can develop automated strategies and compete on equal terms with global financial institutions.

In the pages that follow, we'll explore the key elements of algorithmic trading: from the platforms and programming languages to the builders and VPS servers that enable the continuous and reliable operation of algorithms. Beyond the technical aspects, this book offers a comprehensive overview of how to leverage these tools to maximize market opportunities.

Algorithmic trading isn't just about technology; it's about creativity, strategy, and vision. With this book, we invite you to discover how to design and execute your own strategies, adapt to market dynamics, and ultimately position yourself at the forefront of modern trading.

Welcome to a world where innovation meets finance. This is the starting point to becoming a successful algorithmic trader.

CHAPTER 1

1. Introduction to Algorithmic Trading

1.1. What is algorithmic trading?

Algorithmic trading is based on the creation of algorithms, which are sets of instructions coded in a programming language. These algorithms analyze data in real time, identify market opportunities, and execute trades automatically. The general process includes the following stages:

Strategy Design :

Traders or programmers design a strategy based on specific rules, such as:

Buy an asset if the price crosses above a moving average.

Sell when the price touches a certain resistance.

These rules are based on technical or fundamental analysis, or a combination of both.

Coding :

The strategy is translated into code that can be executed on trading platforms or servers. Common languages include Python, C++, MQL4/MQL5, among others.

Backtesting :

Before implementing the algorithm in the live market, it undergoes a testing process using historical data. This allows the strategy's performance to be evaluated in past scenarios and parameters to be adjusted as needed.

Live Performance :

Once optimized, the algorithm is deployed in the market in real time. It connects directly to trading platforms or broker APIs to send automated orders.

Supervision and Adjustment :

Although the process is automated, traders monitor the algorithm's performance and make adjustments if market conditions change.

1.2. History of algorithmic trading: From early algorithms to today's systems.

Algorithmic trading began to develop in the 1970s with the introduction of the first computers into the financial markets. Initially, these machines were primarily used to calculate theoretical prices and analyze historical data. However, as technology advanced, algorithms began to play an active role in trade execution.

Today, algorithmic trading accounts for a significant portion of trading volume in global markets, especially in assets such as stocks, currencies, futures, and options. High-frequency algorithms (HFT) are an advanced form of algorithmic trading that seeks to exploit micro-market opportunities in milliseconds.

1.3. Advantages and disadvantages of algorithmic trading.

Advantages of Algorithmic Trading

Algorithmic trading offers several advantages that make it a powerful tool for both retail traders and financial institutions:

Fast and Precise Execution :

Algorithms can process vast amounts of data and execute operations in milliseconds, something impossible for humans.

Elimination of Emotions :

Automated trading eliminates the impact of emotions like fear and greed, helping traders follow their strategy in a disciplined manner.

Backtesting Capability :

Algorithms allow strategies to be tested on historical data to assess their viability before applying them in the real market.

Scalability :

Algorithms can manage multiple strategies and markets simultaneously, something that would be impossible for a manual trader.

Time Optimization :

Once the algorithm is developed, it operates autonomously, freeing up time for traders to focus on other activities.

Disadvantages and Challenges of Algorithmic Trading

Despite its advantages, algorithmic trading is not without its challenges:

Technical Complexity :

It requires advanced knowledge of programming, mathematics, and finance, which can be a barrier for beginners.

Risk of Errors :

A mistake in the code or a misinterpretation of data can result in significant losses.

Technological Infrastructure Department :

The success of algorithmic trading depends on fast servers, stable connections, and access to real-time market data.

Intense Competition :

In highly competitive markets, such as high-frequency markets, even a small technological

13

advantage can make the difference between winning and losing.

Risk of Over-Optimization :

Over-adjusting a strategy to historical data can make it ineffective in future market conditions.

1.4. Who can engage in algorithmic trading?

Algorithmic trading, while once reserved for large financial institutions due to high technological costs, is now accessible to a wider range of people thanks to advances in software, accessible trading platforms, and educational resources available online. Below, we explore who can enter this field:

Financial Professionals

Analysts, fund managers, and professional traders are often the primary users of algorithmic trading. Thanks to their advanced knowledge of markets and financial strategies, they use algorithms to optimize their operations, reduce transaction costs, and manage large volumes of assets.

Advantage: These professionals already understand concepts such as market microstructure, risk, and volatility, allowing them to take full advantage of algorithmic tools.

Challenge: Integrating these systems into traditional operations requires technical training in programming and data analysis.

Programmers and Data Scientists

People with programming experience, especially in languages like Python, C++, R, or MQL4/MQL5, have a significant advantage in algorithmic trading. Their ability to build, test, and optimize algorithms makes them key players in this field.

Advantage: They understand how to manipulate large amounts of data and apply mathematical or machine learning models to identify patterns in the market.

Challenge: They must acquire financial knowledge to understand how to apply their technical skills to trading.

Entrepreneurs and Individual Investors

Thanks to accessible trading platforms, individual investors and entrepreneurs can design and use customized algorithmic strategies. This group includes everyone from novice traders to small business owners looking to automate their trading.

Advantage: Access to educational tools, free software, and simulation environments such as MetaTrader, QuantConnect, and NinjaTrader.

Challenge: They require investing time in learning both market fundamentals and basic technical skills.

Students and Academics

Algorithmic trading attracts students of finance, engineering, and mathematics, as well as academic researchers interested in modeling markets or testing economic theories. Many begin their experiments in simulation environments before trading in real markets.

Advantage: Academics can leverage their theoretical knowledge to build advanced prediction and simulation models.

Challenge: Moving from theoretical models to practical systems in real-time market environments can be challenging.

Financial Institutions and Technology Companies

Large companies, including investment banks and hedge funds, are leading the way in the use of algorithmic trading. They have specialized teams that combine financial, technological, and quantitative expertise.

Advantage: Unlimited resources to develop high-frequency systems and complex algorithms.

Challenge: Comply with strict regulations and maintain a competitive advantage over technological rivals.

Basic Requirements for Anyone Interested

Although algorithmic trading is accessible, certain basic skills and tools are required to enter this field:

Financial Literacy: Understanding how financial markets and trading strategies work.

Technical Skills: Familiarity with programming and data analysis.

Platforms and Resources: Access to algorithmic trading software and historical data for testing.

Analytical Mindset: Ability to interpret performance metrics and adjust strategies as needed.

In short, algorithmic trading is accessible to anyone willing to invest the time and effort into acquiring the necessary skills. Whether you come from a financial, technology, or academic background, this field offers unlimited opportunities for those willing to combine logic, data, and technology in financial decision-making.

| Microsoft Azure | Various configurations with Microsoft integration. | Traders who prefer Microsoft services. | Variable according to configuration | Not associated with brokers. |

CHAPTER 2

Fundamentals of the Financial Market

2.1. Operation of financial markets.

Financial markets are platforms where assets such as stocks, bonds, currencies, and derivatives are exchanged, with the purpose of efficiently allocating financial resources among investors, companies, and governments. Their proper functioning is essential for the development of the global economy.

---

1. What are financial markets?

Financial markets are physical or virtual spaces where buyers and sellers transact financial assets. These markets perform three main functions:

Facilitate capital transfers: They connect savers seeking a return on their investments with those in need of project financing.

Provide liquidity: They allow you to buy and sell assets quickly and efficiently.

Pricing: Establishes the value of assets based on supply and demand.

---

2. Types of Financial Markets

Stock Market:

Includes stocks and bonds.

It is where companies and governments obtain financing by issuing financial instruments.

Example: New York Stock Exchange (NYSE), NASDAQ, Madrid Stock Exchange.

Foreign Exchange Market (Forex):

The largest and most liquid market in the world.

In this market, currencies are bought and sold.

Example: EUR/USD, USD/JPY.

Derivatives Market:

Contracts whose value depends on the performance of an underlying asset (stocks, currencies, indices).

Example: Futures, options and swaps.

Raw Materials Market:

Physical assets such as gold, oil, coffee or corn.

Example: NYMEX, ICE.

Money market:

Exchange of short-term debt instruments.

Example: Treasury bills, interbank deposits.

3. Participants in Financial Markets

Investors:

They can be individual or institutional (investment funds, banks).

Your goal is to get a return on your capital.

Issuers:

Companies, governments or entities seeking financing.

Financial Intermediaries:

Banks, brokers, and other entities that facilitate the purchase and sale of assets.

Regulators:

They ensure the fair and efficient functioning of markets.

Example: National Securities Market Commission (CNMV), SEC in the USA.

4. How Transactions Work

Supply and demand:

Asset prices are determined by the interaction between buyers and sellers.

Greater buying interest increases prices, while greater selling interest reduces them.

Market Orders:

Participants submit orders to buy or sell assets through intermediaries or electronic platforms.

Common order types: market orders, limit orders, and stop orders.

Electronic Processing:

Today, most transactions are conducted electronically, which has reduced costs and improved execution speed.

---

5. Regulation of Financial Markets

Objectives of the Regulation:

Protect investors.

Prevent fraudulent activities.

Ensure the stability of the financial system.

Main Rules:

Transparency requirements.

Compliance with anti-money laundering regulations.

Limits to speculation.

---

6. Factors Affecting Market Functioning

Economic Events:

Inflation, interest rates, GDP growth.

Political Events:

Elections, fiscal policies and international conflicts.

Market Sentiment:

Collective psychology of investors (optimism, fear, panic).

Technological Innovation:

Algorithmic trading, artificial intelligence, and blockchain are transforming market dynamics.

---

7. Importance of Efficient Operation

An efficiently operating financial market provides benefits such as:

Better allocation of economic resources.

Reduction of transaction costs.

Greater investor confidence in the financial system.

In short, financial markets are at the heart of the global economy, facilitating the exchange of resources between different economic agents. Their proper functioning depends on a delicate balance between supply and demand, adequate regulation, and technological innovation.

2.2. Types of financial instruments (stocks, currencies, futures, etc.).

Financial instruments are contracts that represent a financial asset or the right to exchange a security between two parties. They can be used for both investment and speculation and are designed to meet the different needs of financial market participants. The main types of financial instruments are described below:

1. Actions

Description:

They represent a fraction of a company's share capital.

Owning a share grants economic rights (dividends) and, in some cases, political rights (voting at shareholder meetings).

Characteristics:

Liquidity: Highly tradable on stock exchanges.

Risk: Its value fluctuates depending on the performance of the company and the market.

Example: Buy Apple (AAPL) stock on the NASDAQ.

Use:

Investors buy stocks with the goal of earning profits from appreciation in value or dividends.

2. Currencies (Forex)

Description:

The foreign exchange market (Forex) is where foreign currencies are bought and sold.

Currency pairs represent the price of one currency in terms of another (e.g. EUR/USD).

Characteristics:

Volatility: High fluctuations due to macroeconomic factors.

Liquidity: It is the largest and most liquid financial market in the world.

24/7 Operation: Available 24 hours a day, five days a week.

Use:

Traders seek profits by speculating on exchange rate movements.

Companies and governments use this market to hedge exchange rate risks in international transactions.

---

3. Bonds

Description:

26

They are debt instruments issued by governments, companies or supranational entities to finance themselves.

The bond buyer acts as a lender who receives interest (coupon) periodically.

Characteristics:

Risk: Varies depending on the issuer's creditworthiness (high-rated bonds such as US Treasuries have low risk).

Maturity: They have a defined maturity date on which the principal is returned.

Use:

Long-term investments and portfolio diversification.

---

4. Futures

Description:

Financial contracts that oblige you to buy or sell an asset at a future date at an agreed price.

The underlying asset can be a commodity (oil, gold) or a financial index (S&P 500).

Characteristics:

Standardization: Traded on organized markets such as the CME.

Leverage: They allow you to control large volumes with a smaller initial investment.

Risk: Highly volatile and speculative.

Use:

Coverage against price or speculation risks.

---

5. Options
Description:

Contracts that grant the right, but not the obligation, to buy (call option) or sell (put option) an asset at a specific price before a certain date.

Characteristics:

Premium: The buyer pays a premium to obtain this right.

Flexibility: Ideal for complex trading strategies.

Risk: Limited to the premium paid for the buyer, but potentially unlimited for the seller.

Use:

Risk management, hedging, and speculation on price movements.

6. Raw Materials (Commodities)

Description:

Commodities such as oil, gold, silver, wheat, and coffee are traded on specialized markets.

Characteristics:

High volatility: Prices are influenced by macroeconomic factors and weather events.

Hedge: Used by producers to protect against price fluctuations.

Use:

Traders speculate on future prices.

Companies use commodity derivatives to manage risks.

7. Derivatives

Description:

Financial instruments whose value depends on the performance of an underlying asset.

Examples: futures, options, swaps.

Characteristics:

Complexity: They require a high degree of financial knowledge.

Leverage: They provide market exposure with a small initial investment.

Use: Risk coverage and speculation.

---

8. Investment Funds

Description:

Collective investment vehicles where investors pool their money to invest in a diversified portfolio of assets.

Characteristics:

Diversification: They reduce risks by investing in multiple assets.

Professional Management: Managed by investment experts.

Common Types:

Fixed-income funds.

Equity funds.

Exchange-traded funds (ETFs).

---

9. Cryptocurrencies

Description:

Digital assets based on blockchain technology.

Example: Bitcoin, Ethereum.

Characteristics:

Extreme volatility: Prices can fluctuate dramatically in short periods.

Innovation: They represent a new asset class with disruptive potential.

Use:

Speculative investment and inflation hedging in some cases.

---

10. Other Instruments

Swaps: Contracts to exchange financial flows (e.g., interest rates).

CFDs (Contracts for Difference): Allow you to speculate on price movements without owning the underlying asset.

Certificates and Warrants: Hybrid instruments for speculation or hedging.

Conclusion

Financial instruments are essential to the functioning of markets, as they allow participants to access various investment, hedging, and speculation opportunities. Each type of instrument is designed to meet specific needs, and their selection depends on the risk profile and objectives of each investor or trader.

2.3. Basic principles of market microstructure

Market microstructure studies how financial markets operate at the operational level, focusing on trading processes, price formation, and the impact of participants' decisions on price behavior. It is a fundamental field for understanding the dynamics behind the buying and selling of assets and how factors such as liquidity, transaction costs, and market structure affect trading performance.

1. Fundamental Concepts of Microstructure

1.1. Liquidity

Definition: The ability of a market to allow the purchase or sale of an asset without causing significant changes in its price.

Liquidity measures:

Depth: Number of orders in the order book at levels close to the current price.

Tightness: Difference between the highest purchase price (bid) and the lowest sale price (ask), known as **the bid-ask spread** .

Resilience: Speed with which the market recovers after large orders.

1.2. Bid-Ask Price

Bid: Highest price a buyer is willing to pay.

Ask: Lowest price at which a seller is willing to sell.

Bid-Ask Spread: The difference between the bid and the ask, representing an implicit cost for traders.

1.3. Price Formation

Prices are formed through the interaction of supply and demand. Market makers or individual participants place orders that determine the traded price.

1.4. Market Efficiency

An efficient market reflects all available information in current asset prices. However, factors such as trading frictions, transaction costs, and information asymmetries can affect this efficiency.

2. Key Components of Microstructure

2.1. Order Book

A record of pending buy and sell orders organized by price level.

Orders:

Market orders: Executed immediately at the best available price.

Limit orders: These are placed at a specific price and executed only if the market reaches that level.

2.2. Types of Participants

Market Makers: They provide liquidity to the market by continuously placing buy and sell orders.

Institutional Traders: They operate large volumes and can significantly influence the price.

Retail Traders: Individual participants who typically operate on a smaller scale.

2.3. Negotiation Mechanisms

Electronic markets: Example: NASDAQ, where transactions are automatic and algorithm-based.

Auction markets: Example: NYSE, where a central auctioneer facilitates trading.

---

3. Transaction Costs

Transaction costs directly influence the profitability of operations and are divided into two types:

3.1. Explicit Costs

Fees charged by financial intermediaries such as brokers or exchanges.

They include commissions, exchange fees, and regulations.

3.2. Implicit Costs

Market Impact: Change in price caused by order size.

Slippage: Difference between the expected price of a transaction and the price at which it is executed.

Spread Cost: Difference between the purchase (ask) and sale (bid) price.

4. Information Asymmetry

It occurs when some market participants possess privileged or more accurate information than others.

Informed traders can take advantage of this information to profit, while uninformed traders may face unfavorable prices.

---

5. Effects of Microstructure on Trading

5.1. Impact on Algorithmic Traders

Algorithms can leverage liquidity and price formation to execute efficient strategies, but they must also consider factors such as slippage and spread costs.

5.2. Importance for Retail Traders

Understanding microstructure concepts allows retail traders to minimize costs, optimize order execution, and avoid losses due to lack of liquidity.

5.3. High Frequency and Microstructure

High-frequency traders (HFT) are particularly sensitive to microstructure, as their success depends on execution speed, order book efficiency, and minimizing implicit costs.

6. Regulation of the Microstructure

Regulators oversee the microstructure to ensure transparency, equal access to information, and the protection of retail participants from unfair practices such as front-running and market manipulation.

Conclusion

Market microstructure is at the heart of financial trading. For traders and algorithms, understanding basic principles such as liquidity, price formation, and transaction costs is essential to executing trades profitably. Beyond being a technical aspect, microstructure influences how financial markets reflect the global economy and facilitate asset exchange.

2.4. Key concepts: Liquidity, Spread, Slippage

In the context of financial markets, **liquidity**, **spread**, and **slippage** are fundamental concepts that directly affect order execution and trading performance. Understanding them is essential for any market participant, whether a retail, institutional, or algorithmic trader.

---

1. Liquidity

Definition:

Liquidity refers to the ease with which an asset can be bought or sold in the market without causing a significant change in its price. A liquid market has a large number of buyers and sellers willing to transact at similar prices.

Liquidity Characteristics:

High Liquidity: Assets such as EUR/USD in Forex or stocks of large companies (Apple, Microsoft) tend to be highly liquid due to the large trading volume.

Low Liquidity: Assets such as small-cap stocks or exotic currencies may have lower liquidity, resulting in more volatile prices.

Importance:

Speed of Execution: In a liquid market, orders are executed quickly.

Price Impact: Liquid markets have a lower risk of a large order significantly altering the asset's price.

Liquidity Measures:

Trading Volume: Number of units of the asset traded in a period of time.

Market Depth: Number of orders in the order book for different price levels.

Bid-Ask Spread: The difference between the nearest buy and ask price, which acts as an indirect indicator of liquidity.

---

2. Spread

Definition:

The spread is the difference between the highest purchase price (bid) and the lowest sale price (ask) in the market. It represents an implicit cost that traders must assume when opening and closing positions.

Spread Types:

Fixed: Common in markets with low volatility or platforms that guarantee constant spreads.

Variable: Fluctuates depending on liquidity, volatility and market conditions.

Practical Example:

Let's say the EUR/USD pair has a **bid** of 1.1050 and an **ask** of 1.1052.

Spread = Ask - Bid = 0.0002 (2 pips).

Factors Affecting the Spread:

Market Volatility: During major economic events, spreads often widen.

Liquidity: Assets with high liquidity tend to have tighter spreads.

Broker: Brokers may add additional commissions to the spread as part of their business model.

Impact of Spread on Trading:

Initial Cost: Each trade starts with a small loss equivalent to the spread.

High Frequency Strategies: High frequency traders (HFT) are especially sensitive to spreads, as they operate on small margins.

---

3. Slippage

Definition:

Slippage occurs when a market order is executed at a different price than expected due to volatility or lack of liquidity at the time of execution.

Types of Slippage:

Positive: The order is executed at a more favorable price than requested (uncommon).

Negative: The order is executed at a less favorable price than requested (more common).

Causes of Slippage:

High Volatility: During economic news announcements, prices can move rapidly.

Low Liquidity: If there are not enough orders in the order book, the system will look for more distant price levels.

Latency: Delays in order execution due to connection speed or technological infrastructure.

Practical Example:

A trader places an order to buy EUR/USD at 1.1050.

Due to a rapid market movement, the order is executed at 1.1053, generating a negative slippage of **3 pips** .

How to Mitigate Slippage:

Use limit orders instead of market orders.

Operate in periods of high liquidity and low volatility.

Select brokers with fast and reliable execution.

Relationship between Liquidity, Spread and Slippage

High Liquidity: Reduces spread and slippage risk, as more orders are available near the current price.

Low Liquidity: Increases the spread and slippage risk, as orders must be executed at more distant prices.

Impact on Algorithmic Trading

In algorithmic trading, these concepts are critical to designing efficient strategies:

Liquidity-Based Models: Algorithms can evaluate market depth to minimize execution costs.

Spread Optimization: Strategies such as arbitrage rely on tight spreads to be profitable.

Slippage Management: High-frequency algorithms are designed to execute orders in milliseconds and reduce the impact of slippage.

Conclusion

Liquidity, spread, and slippage are key concepts for understanding financial market behavior and the implicit costs associated with trading. Proper management of these factors can make the difference between a profitable strategy and a losing one. Both manual and algorithmic traders should incorporate these variables into their analysis to maximize trading efficiency.

CHAPTER 3

Algorithmic Trading Strategies

3.1. Classification of Algorithmic Strategies

Algorithmic trading uses strategies designed to identify and exploit opportunities in financial markets through the use of algorithms. These strategies utilize different approaches to generating profits, depending on the trader's objectives, time horizon, and market conditions. Below are four fundamental types of algorithmic strategies:

1. Market Making

Description:

Market **making** is a strategy that seeks to provide liquidity to the market by placing buy and sell orders simultaneously around the current price. Algorithms generate profit by repeatedly capturing the **bid-ask spread** .

Operation:

The algorithms place limit buy orders (bid) slightly below the current price and sell orders (ask) slightly above.

When these orders are executed, the trader earns profits equal to the spread between the bid and ask.

Characteristics:

Advantage: High frequency of operations with small but constant profits.

Requirement: Liquid and stable markets.

Risk: If the price moves abruptly in one direction, the trader may be left with an unwanted position.

Practical Example:

An algorithm for the EUR/USD pair places buy orders at 1.1045 and sell orders at 1.1048. If both orders are executed, the trader makes a profit of **3 pips** .

---

2. Arbitration

Description:

Arbitrage seeks **to** take advantage of price discrepancies between two or more related markets or assets. These strategies are highly dependent on speed, as discrepancies typically last milliseconds.

Common Types of Arbitration:

Price Arbitrage: Detecting price differences for the same asset in two different markets.

Example: Buying Apple shares on NASDAQ and selling them simultaneously on the London Stock Exchange if there is a price difference.

Statistical Arbitrage: Identify statistical relationships between assets and profit from movements that deviate from the norm.

Example: Arbitrage between correlated stock pairs, such as Coca-Cola and Pepsi.

Merger Arbitrage: Trading assets of companies undergoing merger or acquisition processes, seeking differences between the market price and the expected price after the merger.

Characteristics:

Advantage: Relatively low risk if executed correctly.

Requirement: Low latency and access to multiple markets.

Risk: Errors in statistical analysis or delays in execution can lead to losses.

Practical Example:

An algorithm detects that the price of gold in the New York market is $1,800 per ounce, while in London it is $1,802. It buys in New

York and sells in London, making a profit of $2 per ounce.

---

3. Scalping

Description:

Scalping is a high-frequency strategy that seeks to capture small price movements over **short** periods of time. Scalping algorithms operate multiple times a day, accumulating small but frequent profits.

Operation:

The algorithm identifies opportunities through technical analysis or rapid market signals.

Performs multiple operations lasting from seconds to minutes.

Generally uses high leverage to amplify profits.

Characteristics:

Advantage: Take advantage of intraday volatility and high frequency of opportunities.

Requirement: High execution speed and low transaction costs.

Risk: Exposure to sudden movements against the position.

Practical Example:

An algorithm detects an upward movement in the S&P 500 and opens a long position at 4,100, closing it at 4,102 seconds later, making a profit of 2 points.

---

4. Momentum Trading

Description:

Momentum **trading** exploits the inertia of price movements, trading in the direction of the current trend with the expectation that it will continue in the short to medium term.

Operation:

Algorithms analyze technical indicators such as **RSI (Relative Strength Index)**, **MACD (Moving Average Convergence Divergence)** or moving averages to identify trends.

They enter the market when they detect strong momentum and exit before the movement loses strength.

Characteristics:

Advantage: It is based on market psychology and the tendency to follow existing patterns.

Requirement: Accurate technical analysis and quick adjustments to market changes.

Risk: If the market reverses unexpectedly, losses can be significant.

Practical Example:

An algorithm analyzes the EUR/USD pair and detects that the price has broken through a key resistance at 1.1100 with a significant increase in volume. It opens a long position, expecting the movement to continue, and closes the trade at 1.1115 to capture 15 pips.

Comparison of Strategies

Strategy	Time Horizon	Key Advantage	Main Risk	Example of Use
Market Making	Very short term	Capture the bid-ask spread	Sudden market movements	HFT Algorithmic Trading
Arbitration	Short term	Low risk exposure	Latency or data errors	Differences between markets

49

Strategy	Time Horizon	Key Advantage	Main Risk	Example of Use
Scalping	Very short term	High frequency of benefits	Cumulative transaction costs	Intraday
Momentum Trading	Short to medium term	Follow market trends	Rapid reversals in trends	Swing trading

Conclusion

Algorithmic strategies such as **market making**, **arbitrage**, **scalping,** and **momentum trading** offer varied approaches to participating in the financial markets. Each has associated advantages and risks, making them more suitable for certain trader profiles and market conditions. The selection of a strategy will depend on the trader's objectives, time horizon, and available technological capabilities.

Mean Reversion

Description:

Mean Reversion strategy is based on the principle that asset prices tend to return to their historical average after significant deviations. Algorithms identify these deviations as opportunities to enter long or short positions, hoping the price will return to the mean.

Operation:

A moving average indicator (simple or exponential) is used as a reference for the average price.

Algorithms look for assets that are overbought or oversold relative to their average.

Entries are made when the price deviates significantly (e.g., beyond the Bollinger Bands) and exits occur when the price returns to the mean.

Characteristics:

Advantage: Works well in sideways markets or consolidated ranges.

Risk: In strong trends, the price may continue to move away from the average, generating losses.

Practical Example:

A stock price is trading 5% above its 20-period moving average. The algorithm opens a short position, anticipating that the price will fall toward the moving average, and closes the position when the price touches it.

3.2. Strategies based on technical indicators

Description:

These strategies use mathematical tools applied to historical prices and volumes to predict future market movements. Algorithms analyze these indicators to identify entry and exit signals.

Common Indicators:

Moving Averages:

Crossing moving averages (short and long) to determine trends.

Example: Buy when the 10-day moving average crosses above the 50-day moving average.

Description : It is based on identifying trends using moving averages (simple or exponential). A buy occurs when the price crosses above the moving average, and a sell occurs when it crosses below it.

Risks : May generate false signals in sideways markets.

Chances of Success : High in trending markets.

Resources : Historical price data, backtesting tools, ability to adjust parameters such as averaging periods.

Platform/Language : MetaTrader 5 (MQL5).

Technical Details :

Indicators : Simple moving average (SMA) or exponential moving average (EMA).

Conditions :

Buy: Price crosses above the moving average.

Sell: Price crosses below the moving average.

Platform : MetaTrader 5.

Language : MQL5.

Sample Code :

mql5

Copy code

```
if (Close[1] > iMA(NULL, 0, 20, 0, MODE_SMA, PRICE_CLOSE, 0)) {
// Buys
SendOrder(OP_BUY, 0.1);
```

```
} else if (Close[1] < iMA(NULL, 0, 20, 0, MODE_SMA, PRICE_CLOSE, 0)) {
// Sale
SendOrder(OP_SELL, 0.1);
}
```

RSI (Relative Strength Index):

Identify overbought (>70) and oversold (<30) levels.

MACD (Moving Average Convergence/Divergence):

Buy/sell signals based on line crossovers and divergences.

Bollinger Bands:

Used to identify volatility levels; entries near the outer bands and exits near the midline.

Description : Trade based on the price position relative to the upper and lower Bollinger bands, looking for reversals.

Risks : False signals in highly volatile markets.

Chances of Success : High in markets with defined ranges.

Resources : Technical volatility indicators.

Platform/Language : MetaTrader 5 (MQL5).

Technical Details :

Indicators : Bollinger Bands.

Conditions :

Purchase: Price touches lower band.

Sale: Price touches upper band.

Platform : MetaTrader 5.

Sample Code :

mql5

Copy code

```
double upperBand, lowerBand;
iBands(NULL, 0, 20, 2, 0, PRICE_CLOSE, upperBand, lowerBand);
if (Close[1] < lowerBand) {
SendOrder(OP_BUY, 0.1);
} else if (Close[1] > upperBand) {
SendOrder(OP_SELL, 0.1);
}
```

Advantages:

They offer objective and replicable rules.

Easy to combine with other indicators.

Risks:

They can generate false signals in volatile or directionless markets.

Practical Example:

An algorithm analyzes the RSI of an index like the S&P 500. When the RSI falls below 30, it opens a buy position in anticipation of a technical rebound.

5. Trading with Elliott Waves

Description : Use Elliott wave patterns to identify market cycles and future predictions.

Risks : Subjective interpretation of the waves.

Chances of Success : Depends on the operator's experience.

Resources : Technical analysis tools and Elliott wave training.

Platform/Language : TradingView (Pine Script).

Technical Details :

Tools : Manual detection or specialized software.

Platform : TradingView.

Language : Pine Script.

6. Crypto Arbitrage Strategies

Description : Buy cryptocurrencies on one platform where they are cheaper and sell them on another where they are more expensive.

Risks : Risk of price slippage and transfer times.

Chances of Success : High in fragmented markets.

Resources : Cryptocurrency exchange API.

Platform/Language : Python with API connection libraries.

Technical Details :

Requirements : Exchange APIs, initial capital.

Conditions :

Detect price differences between exchanges.

Sample Code :

python

Copy code

```
price_binance = get_price('BTC', 'Binance')
price_coinbase = get_price('BTC', 'Coinbase')

if price_binance < price_coinbase:
buy('BTC', 'Binance')
sell('BTC', 'Coinbase')
```

3.3. Event-based strategies (news, earnings reports)

Description:

These strategies exploit price movements triggered by fundamental events, such as corporate earnings announcements, interest rate changes, or macroeconomic data.

Operation:

Algorithms track real-time news sources or economic calendars.

They analyze the historical impact of similar events to predict market reaction.

Positions are opened and closed quickly after the event to take advantage of volatility.

Common Types of Events:

Earnings Reports:

Operations based on positive or negative surprises in quarterly results.

Monetary Policy:

Currency and bond movements following central bank decisions.

Macroeconomic Data:

Inflation, employment, or GDP that affect stock market indices or currencies.

Advantages:

High profit potential in short periods.

Based on specific and quantifiable events.

Risks:

High volatility can cause significant slippage.

It's difficult to predict market reactions, as news is sometimes "discounted."

Practical Example:

An algorithm detects that a company has exceeded its earnings expectations by 20%. It immediately opens a buy position on the stock, holding it for a few hours to take advantage of the momentum.

3.4. High Frequency Trading (HFT) Strategies

Description:

High-Frequency Trading (HFT) uses algorithms to execute large numbers of trades in milliseconds. These strategies focus on exploiting tiny price differences or temporary imbalances in the market.

Types of HFT Strategies:

Arbitration:

Detect and exploit price discrepancies between different markets or assets.

Market Making:

Provide liquidity by capturing the bid-ask spread.

Intraday Momentum:

Detect rapid market movements and ride the trend for a short period.

Characteristics:

Speed: HFT algorithms operate in microseconds.

Volume: They carry out thousands of operations daily, accumulating small profits.

Infrastructure: They require low-latency servers and proximity to the exchanges.

Advantages:

They generate consistent profits by taking advantage of market inefficiencies.

They are not exposed to prolonged risks due to their ultra-short focus.

Risks:

Intense competition with other HFT algorithms.

Dependence on advanced and expensive technology.

Stricter regulations in several countries.

Practical Example:

An algorithm detects that the price of a stock on the New York market is misaligned with the price of the same ETF in London by a few microseconds. It executes a buy in New York and a sell in London, closing both positions for an instant profit.

3.5. Machine Learning-Based Strategies

Description : Uses predictive models trained on historical data to anticipate price movements.

Risks : Overfitting to historical data.

Chances of Success : High if the data is sufficient and relevant.

Resources : Knowledge of machine learning, modeling tools such as TensorFlow or PyTorch.

Platform/Language : Python.

Technical Details :

Tools : Scikit-learn, TensorFlow.

Data : Historical prices, volume, etc.

Conditions :

Train model with past data.

Predict future movements.

Sample Code :

python

Copy code

```
from sklearn.ensemble import RandomForestClassifier
model = RandomForestClassifier()

X_train = data[['Open', 'High', 'Low', 'Close']].values
y_train = data['Target'].values
model.fit(X_train, y_train)
prediction = model.predict(new_data)
```

Conclusion

These algorithmic strategies—Mean Reversion, technical indicator-based, event-based, and HFT—offer varied approaches to trading in the financial markets. Each strategy has its own advantages, requirements, and risks, and their selection depends on factors such as the trader's time horizon, risk profile, and technological resources.

CHAPTER 4

Design and Development of Algorithms

4.1. Components of an algorithmic system:

Entry, risk management and exit.

4.1. Components of an algorithmic system: Input, Risk Management and Output

An efficient algorithmic trading system is built on three fundamental pillars: **entry** , **risk management** , and **exit** . Each of these components plays an essential role in trade execution and performance. The following details how these elements are designed and implemented:

1. Entrance

The input determines when and under what conditions the algorithm opens a market position. This component is based on predefined criteria that can be technical, fundamental, statistical, or a combination of these.

Key elements of the entry:

Entry Criteria:

Define specific rules for starting an operation.

Example: Open a buy position when the price crosses above the 50-period moving average.

Signal Sources:

Technical Indicators: RSI, MACD, Bollinger Bands, moving averages.

Key Events: Economic news, earnings reports.

Statistical Models: Analysis of historical patterns.

Filters:

Additional rules to avoid false signals.

Example: Only trade during sessions with high liquidity, such as the opening of the New York market.

Common mistakes:

Defining entry criteria that are too broad, which can generate false signals.

Ignoring market context, such as volatility or macroeconomic conditions.

Practical Example:

An algorithmic trading system might have this rule:

Condition: Open a buy position if the RSI is below 30 (overbought) and the price crosses above the 20-period moving average.

Action: Submit a purchase order with a defined lot size.

---

2. Risk Management

Risk management is the most critical component of the system, designed to limit losses, protect capital, and ensure the long-term sustainability of the system.

Key elements of risk management:

Position Sizing:

Determine how much capital will be allocated to each operation.

Example: Use 1% of total capital per trade, which limits exposure in case of loss.

Stop Loss:

Predefined level at which the position will be automatically closed if the price moves against it.

Example: Placing a Stop Loss 20 pips from the entry price in Forex.

Take Profit:

Level at which the system will automatically close a position to lock in profits.

Example: Exit a trade when you have made a profit of 30 pips.

Risk-Benefit Ratio (R:B):

Relationship between the risk assumed and the expected benefit.

Example: A system with an R:B of 1:2 risks 1 currency unit to gain 2.

Maximum Daily Losses:

Limit losses allowed per day or week to avoid trading in adverse conditions.

Example: Stop the system if you lose 5% of your capital in one day.

Diversification:

Avoid concentrating operations in a single asset or market.

Example: Trading in multiple currency pairs or financial instruments.

Common mistakes:

Failure to set a Stop Loss, which can result in significant losses.

Using inconsistent position sizes or overleveraging.

Practical Example:

A system can assign a lot size based on equity and volatility:

Position Size Calculation: Equity = $10,000, Risk per trade = 1%, Stop Loss = 50 pips. The lot size will be adjusted to avoid a loss of $100.

---

3. Exit

The exit strategy defines when and how the system closes a position. A proper exit strategy can maximize profits and limit losses, even if the entry wasn't perfect.

Key elements of the output:

Exit Rules:

Close positions based on technical criteria, such as indicator crossovers or support/resistance levels.

Example: Exit if price crosses below the 20-period moving average.

Trailing Stop:

A dynamic Stop Loss that moves in favor of the position as the price advances.

Example: Place a trailing stop that follows the price at a distance of 20 pips.

Time Based Exit:

Close positions after a specific period of time.

Example: Exit at the end of the market session.

Closing due to Market Conditions:

Close all positions if volatility increases dramatically or if unexpected events are announced.

Common mistakes:

Not using a defined exit plan, which can lead to holding losing positions for too long.

Exit prematurely, limiting profit potential.

Practical Example:

A system with trailing stop can automatically adjust the output level:

Rule: If the price moves 50 pips in favor, the Stop Loss is adjusted to ensure 30 pips of profit.

General Flow of an Algorithmic System

Input: The algorithm identifies a signal based on predefined criteria.

Execution: Place an order with the calculated position size.

Risk Management: Apply Stop Loss and Take Profit according to the rules.

Exit: Close the position according to the exit strategy (crosses, trailing stop or time).

Conclusion

A successful algorithmic system combines accurate entry, sound risk management, and efficient exit strategies. These components work together to maximize profits and minimize losses, ensuring the system's sustainability under varying market conditions.

4.2. Popular programming languages in algorithmic trading:

Algorithmic trading requires programming languages capable of processing financial data, implementing complex strategies, and executing orders in real time. Some languages stand out for their flexibility, speed, or integration with trading platforms. Below, we analyze the most popular languages used in algorithmic trading:

1. Python

Description:

Python is one of the most widely used languages in algorithmic trading due to its simplicity, versatility, and wide variety of specialized libraries.

Advantages:

Easy to learn: Ideal for beginners thanks to its intuitive syntax.

Financial Libraries:

Pandas: For data analysis.

NumPy: For numerical calculations.

Matplotlib/Plotly: For data visualization.

Backtrader: For backtesting strategies.

Integration: Compatible with APIs from trading platforms such as Interactive Brokers, Alpaca, and Binance.

Machine Learning and AI: Compatible with advanced libraries such as TensorFlow, Keras, and Scikit-learn.

Disadvantages:

Slower than languages like C++ for high-frequency tasks.

It is not specifically designed for real-time trading environments.

Example of Use:

Create a basic moving average crossover system:

```
import pandas as pd
import numpy as np

# Load historical data
data = pd.read_csv("historic_data.csv")

# Calculate moving averages
data['MA50'] = data['Close'].rolling(window=50).mean()
data['MA200'] = data['Close'].rolling(window=200).mean()

# Buy/Sell Signal
data['Signal'] = np.where(data['MA50'] > data['MA200'], 1, -1)

print(data[['Close', 'MA50', 'MA200', 'Signal']])
```

---

2. MQL4/MQL5
Description:

MQL4 and MQL5 are languages specifically for the MetaTrader platform, widely used in Forex and CFDs. They are designed for programming **Expert Advisors (EAs)**, custom indicators, and scripts.

Advantages:

Direct Integration: Designed exclusively for MetaTrader, making it easy to execute strategies directly within the platform.

Optimization and Backtesting: Integrated tools for testing and fine-tuning strategies.

Complete Automation: Allows you to open, close and manage positions without manual intervention.

Compatibility: MQL4 is used in MetaTrader 4 and MQL5 in MetaTrader 5, the latter being more powerful and versatile.

Disadvantages:

Specialized languages, not applicable outside the MetaTrader ecosystem.

They require knowledge of specific MetaTrader structures.

Example of Use:

A basic EA to open a buy position when the price crosses the 50-period moving average:

input int MA_Period = 50; // Period of the moving average

```
double ma_value;

// Main function of the EA
void OnTick()
{
ma_value = iMA(NULL, 0, MA_Period, 0, MODE_SMA, PRICE_CLOSE, 0);

if (Close[0] > ma_value) {
if (PositionsTotal() == 0) {
// Open buy position
trade.Buy(0.1, Symbol());
}
}
}
```

3. R

Description:

R is a language designed for statistical analysis and data mining. It is primarily used for developing predictive models and analyzing large financial data sets.

Advantages:

Advanced Analytics: Ideal for modeling financial data and performing simulations.

Visualization: Libraries such as **ggplot2** and **Shiny** to create interactive charts and dashboards.

Extensibility: Libraries such as **quantmod** and **TTR** for technical analysis.

Disadvantages:

It is not optimized for real-time execution.

Less intuitive than Python for beginners.

Example of Use:

Calculate basic technical indicators:

library(quantmod)

Download data

getSymbols("AAPL", src = "yahoo", from = "2022-01-01", to = "2022-12-31")

```
# Calculate moving averages
AAPL$MA50 <- SMA(Cl(AAPL), n = 50)
AAPL$MA200 <- SMA(Cl(AAPL), n = 200)

# Graph
chartSeries(AAPL, TA = "addSMA(50, col='red'); addSMA(200, col='blue')")
```

4. C++

Description:

C++ is a high-performance language used primarily in **high-frequency trading (HFT) strategies** and institutional trading systems that require speed and accuracy.

Advantages:

Speed: Ideal for tasks that demand low latency and high frequency.

Total Control: Allows you to manage memory and system resources, optimizing performance.

Reliability: Widely used in critical financial systems such as market making and arbitrage.

Disadvantages:

Steep learning curve.

Fewer out-of-the-box financial libraries compared to Python.

Example of Use:

Basic snippet for calculating a moving average:

```cpp
#include <iostream>
#include <vector>
#include <numeric>
```

```cpp
double calculateSMA(const std::vector<double>& prices, int period) {
if (prices.size() < period) return -1; // Not enough data
return std::accumulate(prices.end() - period, prices.end(), 0.0) / period;
}

int main() {
std::vector<double> prices = {1.1, 1.2, 1.3, 1.4, 1.5}; // Example prices
int period = 3;
std::cout << "SMA: " << calculateSMA(prices, period) << std::endl;
return 0;
}
```

Comparison

Language	Ease of Use	Speed	Common Use	Ideal For
Python	High	Average	Analysis, backtesting, AI	Retail traders and

Language	Ease of Use	Speed	Common Use	Ideal For
				researchers
MQL4/5	Average	High	MetaTrader	Forex and CFD Traders
R	Average	Low	Statistical modeling, simulations	Analysts and academics
C++	Low	Very high	High Frequency Systems (HFT)	Financial institutions

Conclusion

The ideal language for algorithmic trading depends on the trader's objective and the available technological resources. Python is ideal for research and testing, MQL4/5 for integrating strategies directly into MetaTrader, R for advanced data analysis, and C++ for high-frequency systems where speed is crucial.

4.3. Introduction to trading APIs and platforms (MetaTrader, Interactive Brokers).

Trading APIs and trading platforms are fundamental tools in algorithmic trading, allowing traders to automate strategies, analyze data, and execute orders directly in the financial markets. Below is an introduction to two of the most popular platforms and their respective APIs: MetaTrader and Interactive Brokers.

1. What is a Trading API?

A trading API (Application Programming Interface) is a set of tools and protocols that allow developers to interact with trading platforms. These APIs facilitate:

Access to market data: Real-time prices, historical data, and market depth.

Order execution: Sending, modifying and canceling orders.

Account Management: Check balances, margins, and open positions.

Automation: Integrate algorithmic trading strategies with the platform system.

---

2. MetaTrader (MQL4/MQL5)

MetaTrader is one of the most popular platforms in the foreign exchange (Forex) and contracts for difference (CFD) markets. It offers an integrated API in the form of its own programming languages: MQL4 (MetaTrader 4) and MQL5 (MetaTrader 5).

MetaTrader API Features:

Integrated Language (MQL4/MQL5):

Designed specifically for programming strategies (Expert Advisors), custom indicators and scripts.

It offers tools for technical analysis, risk management, and order execution.

Backtesting and Optimization:

MetaTrader includes a simulator for testing strategies on historical data and adjusting parameters.

Automatic Execution of Strategies:

The algorithms run directly on the platform without the need for integration with external systems.

Access to Market Data:

Real-time data, historical quotes, and analysis tools.

Example of use in MQL5:

Open a buy order in MetaTrader 5:

```
#include <Trade/Trade.mqh>


input double LotSize = 0.1;
```

```
CTrade trade;

void OnTick()
{
double ma = iMA(NULL, 0, 20, 0, MODE_SMA, PRICE_CLOSE, 0); // 20-period moving average

if (Close[0] > ma && PositionsTotal() == 0) {
trade.Buy(LotSize, Symbol());
}
}
```

Advantages of MetaTrader:

Easy to use: Ideal for traders new to algorithmic trading.

Global Support: Large user base and compatible brokers.

Backtesting: Integrated directly into the platform.

Disadvantages:

Limited to brokers that support MetaTrader.

Less flexible than generic APIs like Python for advanced strategies.

3. Interactive Brokers (IBKR)

Interactive Brokers is a platform that allows you to trade a wide range of assets, including stocks, options, futures, forex, and more. Its API, known as the IBKR API , offers support for several programming languages.

Interactive Brokers API Features:

Multilanguage Support:

Compatible with Python , Java , C++ , and R.

Allows developers to choose the language that best suits their needs.

Global Coverage:

Access to more than 135 markets worldwide.

Flexibility:

Possibility to fully customize trading strategies.

Access to advanced market data, market depth, and real-time analysis.

Paper Trading:

Simulation accounts to test strategies risk-free.

Example of use in Python with IBKR API:

Obtain market data and place a buy order:

from ib_insync import *

```python
# Connecting to the API
ib = IB()
ib.connect('127.0.0.1', 7497, clientId=1)

# Request market data
contract = Stock('AAPL', 'SMART', 'USD')
ib.qualifyContracts(contract)
data = ib.reqMktData(contract)

# Place a purchase order
order = MarketOrder('BUY', 10) # Buy 10 shares
trade = ib.placeOrder(contract, order)

# Close the connection
ib.disconnect()
```

Advantages of Interactive Brokers:

Versatility: Supports multiple assets and programming languages.

Institutional Access: Ideal for advanced traders and large volumes.

Paper Trading: Excellent for testing strategies risk-free.

Disadvantages:

Steeper learning curve for beginners.

Dependence on external servers, which can introduce latency.

Comparison between MetaTrader and Interactive Brokers

Feature	MetaTrader	Interactive Brokers
Operable Assets	Forex, CFD	Stocks, options, futures, currencies, bonds
Programming language	MQL4/MQL5	Python, Java, C++, R
Integrated Platform	Yeah	No (requires integration)
Backtesting	Yes, integrated	Needs implementation
Ease of Use	High (for Forex/CFD)	Moderate (for multiple markets)

Feature	MetaTrader	Interactive Brokers
Flexibility	Limited to the MT ecosystem	High (supports complex strategies)

Conclusion

The MetaTrader and Interactive Brokers APIs represent two distinct approaches to algorithmic trading. MetaTrader is ideal for retail traders focused on Forex and CFDs, while Interactive Brokers offers a robust solution for diversified, multi-asset strategies in a professional environment. The choice depends on the trader's needs and the scope of their strategies.

4.4. Practical example: Writing a basic trading algorithm

The following describes how to create a basic trading algorithm that implements a simple **moving average crossover strategy** . This example will illustrate the essential steps for developing an automated trading system, from strategy definition to order execution.

Chosen Strategy: Moving Average Crossover

The moving average crossover strategy is based on comparing two moving averages:

Fast Moving Average (Fast MA): Calculated with a short period, such as 10.

Slow Moving Average (Slow MA): Calculated with a longer period, such as 50.

Rules:

Buy: When the fast MA crosses above the slow MA.

Sell: When the fast MA crosses below the slow MA.

All positions are closed if the signal is reversed.

Platform and Language: MetaTrader 5 (MQL5)

Code Structure

The code includes the following components:

Initialization of variables and configuration of strategy parameters.

Calculation of moving averages.

Implementation of entry and exit rules.

Execution of orders based on the generated signals.

MQL5 Code: Moving Average Crossover

```
// Import the library for business operations
#include <Trade\Trade.mqh>

// Create an object for executing operations
CTrade trade;

// EA Parameters
input int Fast_MA_Period = 10; // Period of the fast average
input int Slow_MA_Period = 50; // Slow average period
input double LotSize = 0.1; // Lot size
```

```
input double StopLoss = 20; // Stop Loss in points
input double TakeProfit = 50; // Take Profit in points

// Global variables
double Fast_MA, Slow_MA;

// Main function: executed on every tick
void OnTick()
{
// Calculate moving averages
Fast_MA = iMA(NULL, 0, Fast_MA_Period, 0, MODE_SMA, PRICE_CLOSE, 0);
Slow_MA = iMA(NULL, 0, Slow_MA_Period, 0, MODE_SMA, PRICE_CLOSE, 0);

// Purchase rule
if (Fast_MA > Slow_MA && PositionsTotal() == 0) {
trade.Buy(LotSize, NULL, Ask, StopLoss, TakeProfit);
}
```

// Sale rule

if (Fast_MA < Slow_MA && PositionsTotal() == 0) {

trade.Sell(LotSize, NULL, Bid, StopLoss, TakeProfit);

}

}

Explanation of the Code

Import Libraries:

The Trade.mqh library allows you to manage operations such as opening and closing positions.

Define Parameters:

Fast_MA_Period and **Slow_MA_Period** set the periods of the moving averages.

LotSize: Position size in lots.

StopLoss and TakeProfit: Automatic closing levels to limit losses and secure profits.

Calculate Moving Averages:

The iMA function calculates the simple moving average based on the closing price.

Buy/Sell Rules:

If the **fast MA** crosses above the **slow MA** and there are no open positions, the algorithm opens a buy position.

If the **fast MA** crosses below the **slow MA**, a sell position is opened.

Execution and Testing
Steps to Run the EA:
Open MetaTrader 5.

Create a new script or Expert Advisor using the **MetaEditor** .

Copy and paste the code above.

Save and compile the code.

Apply the EA to a chart of any currency pair (e.g. EUR/USD).

Backtesting:

Use the strategy tester built into MetaTrader to test the EA on historical data.

Adjust parameters such as moving average periods, lot size, or stop loss and take profit levels to optimize performance.

Alternative Example: Python with the Interactive Brokers API

If you prefer a more general approach, here's a Python example that implements the same moving average crossover strategy using the Interactive Brokers API.

```python
from ib_insync import *

# Connect to Interactive Brokers
ib = IB()
ib.connect('127.0.0.1', 7497, clientId=1)

# Configure the contract (e.g., AAPL)
contract = Stock('AAPL', 'SMART', 'USD')
ib.qualifyContracts(contract)

# Download historical data
data = ib.reqHistoricalData(contract, endDateTime='', durationStr='1 D', barSizeSetting='1 min', whatToShow='MIDPOINT', useRTH=True)

# Calculate moving averages
```

```
data['MA10'] = data['close'].rolling(window=10).mean()
data['MA50'] = data['close'].rolling(window=50).mean()

# Implement crossover rules
if data['MA10'].iloc[-1] > data['MA50'].iloc[-1]:
    order = MarketOrder('BUY', 10) # Buy 10 shares
    ib.placeOrder(contract, order)
elif data['MA10'].iloc[-1] < data['MA50'].iloc[-1]:
    order = MarketOrder('SELL', 10) # Sell 10 shares
    ib.placeOrder(contract, order)

ib.disconnect()
```

Conclusion

This basic example shows how to implement a simple trading algorithm using MetaTrader 5 and MQL5 or Python with Interactive Brokers. Both approaches illustrate the key elements of an algorithmic system: **signal identification,**

order execution, and risk management . From this model, more advanced features such as trailing stops, multiple indicators, and automatic optimization can be added.

CHAPTER 5

5. Data Analysis and Machine Learning in Trading

Data analytics and machine learning are transforming trading by providing advanced tools for analyzing large volumes of information and building adaptive strategies. This chapter explores how historical data and machine learning techniques are used to develop predictive models and optimize trading in financial markets.

5.1. Using Historical Data to Build Strategies

Importance of Historical Data:

Historical data is the foundation for building and testing trading strategies. Analyzing past patterns allows you to identify relationships and trends that can be exploited in the future.

Steps in Historical Data Analysis:

Harvest:

Obtain price, volume, indicator, and historical event data from platforms like MetaTrader, Yahoo Finance, or Bloomberg.

Cleaning:

Correct missing or inconsistent data and adjust prices for dividends or splits.

Exploration:

Identify patterns, correlations, and anomalies using graphs and descriptive statistics.

Building Strategies:

Create rules based on observed patterns, such as moving average crossovers or overbought/oversold indicators.

Practical Example:

Using Python to calculate moving averages on historical data:

```python
import pandas as pd
import yfinance as yf

# Download historical data
data = yf.download('AAPL', start='2022-01-01', end='2023-01-01')

# Calculate moving averages
data['MA50'] = data['Close'].rolling(window=50).mean()
data['MA200'] = data['Close'].rolling(window=200).mean()
```

```
# Identify signs
data['Signal'] = data['MA50'] > data['MA200']
print(data.tail())
```

5.2. Introduction to Machine Learning for Trading

Machine learning enables the construction of models capable of identifying complex patterns in data and dynamically adapting to market conditions.

Why use Machine Learning in Trading?

Prediction: Improve the accuracy of price and trend forecasting.

Adaptation: Adjust strategies in real time based on new data.

Automation: Creating autonomous decision-making systems.

Types of Machine Learning:

Supervised:

The model is trained with labeled data to predict future values.

Example: Predicting the closing price of a stock based on historical data.

Unsupervised:

Identify hidden patterns in unlabeled data.

Example: Grouping assets with similar behaviors.

Reinforcement Learning:

Algorithms that learn through trial and error to maximize profits.

Example: Algorithmic trading systems that dynamically adjust parameters.

5.3. Common Models: Regression, Neural Networks, Decision Trees

1. Regression:

Purpose: To model the relationship between independent variables (input factors) and dependent variables (price).

Use: Predict continuous values, such as the closing price of an asset.

Example:

Use linear regression to estimate the impact of volume on price.

2. Neural Networks:

Purpose: To mimic the functioning of the human brain to identify non-linear patterns.

Guys:

Multilayer Perceptron Networks (MLP): For classification or regression problems.

Recurrent Neural Networks (RNN): Specialized in time series, such as historical prices.

Use: Predict complex and dynamic market trends.

Example:

Using a neural network to predict the price of Bitcoin based on historical data.

3. Decision Trees:

Purpose: To create a tree-shaped decision model that classifies or predicts values based on input variables.

Advantages: Easy to interpret and quick to train.

Example:

Deciding whether to buy, sell, or hold a stock based on indicators such as RSI or moving averages.

Sample Code (Regression with Python):

```
from sklearn.linear_model import LinearRegression
from sklearn.model_selection import train_test_split
```

```python
import pandas as pd

# Load historical data
data = pd.read_csv('data.csv')

# Independent and dependent variables
X = data[['Volume', 'Open', 'High', 'Low']]
y = data['Close']

# Split data into training and testing
X_train, X_test, y_train, y_test = train_test_split(X, y, test_size=0.2)

# Train model
model = LinearRegression()
model.fit(X_train, y_train)

# Prediction
predictions = model.predict(X_test)
print(predictions)
```

5.4. How to Avoid Overfitting in Predictive Models

Overfitting occurs when a model overfits the training data, losing generalization ability.

Tips to Avoid Overfitting:

Splitting the Data:

Separate the data into training, validation, and test sets.

Simplify the Model:

Avoid using too many irrelevant parameters or features.

Regularization:

Use techniques such as L1 or L2 to penalize extreme coefficients.

Cross-Validation:

Validate the model on multiple data subsets.

Expand the Dataset:

Increase the size of the data with additional information or synthetic data generation techniques.

Practical Example of Cross-Validation:

from sklearn.model_selection import cross_val_score

from sklearn.ensemble import RandomForestRegressor

```
# Random Forest Model
model = RandomForestRegressor()

# Cross-evaluation
scores = cross_val_score(model, X, y, cv=5)
print("Cross-validation scores:", scores)
```

Conclusion

Data analysis and machine learning offer advanced tools for optimizing trading. From the use of historical data to the implementation of predictive models such as neural networks or decision trees, these techniques allow for identifying opportunities and improving the accuracy of strategies. However, avoiding problems such as overfitting is crucial to ensuring the effectiveness of models on real data.

CHAPTER 6

Evaluation and Optimization of Strategies

6. Evaluation and Optimization of Strategies

The evaluation and optimization of trading strategies are crucial steps to ensure the effectiveness of an algorithmic system before its implementation in real markets. This process includes backtesting, parameter optimization, and strategy validation through real-time simulations (paper trading).

6.1. Backtesting

Backtesting involves testing a trading strategy on historical data to evaluate its performance under different market conditions.

1. How to Test with Historical Data

Data Collection:

Get accurate historical data including open, close, high, low, and volume prices.

Common sources: MetaTrader, Yahoo Finance, Interactive Brokers API.

Data Cleansing:

Eliminate duplicate data, missing or inconsistent values.

Adjust prices for dividends or splits in the case of shares.

Implementation of the Strategy:

Codify the entry and exit rules of the strategy.

Simulate the system on historical data to generate buy and sell signals.

Results:

Calculate key metrics (detailed below) to evaluate the strategy.

Practical Example: Moving Average Crossover Backtesting (Python):

```python
import pandas as pd

# Load historical data
data = pd.read_csv('historical_data.csv')

# Calculate moving averages
data['MA50'] = data['Close'].rolling(window=50).mean()
data['MA200'] = data['Close'].rolling(window=200).mean()
```

```python
# Buy/Sell Signals
data['Signal'] = 0
data.loc[data['MA50'] > data['MA200'], 'Signal'] = 1
data.loc[data['MA50'] <= data['MA200'], 'Signal'] = -1

# Calculate yields
data['Daily Return'] = data['Close'].pct_change()
data['Strategy Return'] = data['Signal'].shift(1) * data['Daily Return']

# Evaluate performance
total_return = data['Strategy Return'].cumsum().iloc[-1]
print(f"Total return: {total_return:.2%}")
```

2. Key Metrics for Evaluating a Trading System

Total Yield:

Accumulated profit or loss of the strategy in the period analyzed.

Maximum Drawdown:

The biggest drop from a capital peak to a valley.

Measures the risk associated with the strategy.

Sharpe ratio:

Risk-adjusted return (average return divided by standard deviation).

Formula: $Sharpe = \frac{R - R_f}{\sigma}$

Win Rate:

Percentage of profitable operations.

Risk-Benefit Ratio (R:B):

Average size of wins versus average size of losses.

6.2. Parameter Optimization

1. Sensitivity Analysis

Sensitivity analysis evaluates how changes in strategy parameters affect its performance. This ensures that the strategy is robust and not dependent on specific values.

Steps:

Identify key parameters (e.g., moving average periods).

Try different combinations of parameters in backtesting.

Analyze how key metrics vary with each combination.

Practical Example:

```
import itertools

# Parameters to test
fast_ma_range = range(10, 31, 5)
slow_ma_range = range(50, 101, 10)

# Parameter combinations
for fast, slow in itertools.product(fast_ma_range, slow_ma_range):
    data['Fast_MA'] = data['Close'].rolling(window=fast).mean()
    data['Slow_MA'] = data['Close'].rolling(window=slow).mean()
    # Evaluate the strategy with these parameters...
```

2. Overfitting Detection

Overfitting occurs when a strategy performs exceptionally well on historical data, but fails on new data because it is too tightly tuned to specific patterns from the past.

How to Avoid It:

Split the data into training and test sets.

Use cross-validation to evaluate the strategy on different subsets of the data.

Prefer simple strategies with fewer parameters.

Overfitting Indicators:

Significantly better results on training data versus test data.

The strategy works well only in certain periods or assets.

6.3. Real-Time Testing (Paper Trading)

Paper trading involves testing a strategy in real time using a simulated account. This allows you to validate its performance without risking real money.

Benefits of Paper Trading:

Test the execution of the strategy under real market conditions.

Detect errors in the algorithm logic or latency problems.

Evaluate the impact of transaction costs such as spread or slippage.

Common Tools for Paper Trading:

MetaTrader: Use demo accounts to run Expert Advisors in real market conditions.

Interactive Brokers API: Implement strategies with real-time data in a simulation account.

Simulation Platforms: Such as QuantConnect or Alpaca, which offer environments for paper trading.

Paper Trading Example (Python and Interactive Brokers):

from ib_insync import *

# Connecting to the IBKR API
ib = IB()
ib.connect('127.0.0.1', 7497, clientId=1)

```
# Contract Configuration
contract = Stock('AAPL', 'SMART', 'USD')
ib.qualifyContracts(contract)

# Monitor price in real time
while True:
    market_data = ib.reqMktData(contract)
    print(f"Current price: {market_data.last}")
    # Trading logic...
```

Conclusion

Backtesting, parameter optimization, and paper trading are fundamental steps in the development of algorithmic strategies. Thorough testing and parameter tuning ensure strategies are robust and profitable, while real-time testing allows you to validate their performance in real-world environments before committing capital.

CHAPTER 7

Implementation and Execution

Implementing and running a live algorithmic trading system requires a robust architecture, efficient latency management, and a solid focus on risk management. This chapter details how to build a system for real-time trading and how to ensure its effectiveness and sustainability.

7.1. Architecture for a Live Trading System

The architecture of an algorithmic trading system must be modular, scalable, and resilient, allowing for the seamless integration of data, strategies, and order execution.

Components of Architecture:

Data Source:

Real-time data provider for prices, volumes, and news.

Example: MetaTrader APIs, Interactive Brokers, or providers like Bloomberg or Alpha Vantage.

Strategy Engine:

Module that executes trading logic based on the signals generated by the strategy.

It can include rules based on technical analysis, machine learning, or events.

Execution Engine:

Responsible for sending, modifying, and canceling orders to the broker or exchange.

You should minimize latency to ensure fast execution.

Risk Management:

Control of exposure limits, Stop Loss, Take Profit and position size.

Monitoring and Logging:

Monitor key metrics, executed orders, and potential errors in real time.

Record data for later analysis.

User Interface (optional):

Panel to view performance, modify parameters and stop the system if necessary.

Simplified Flowchart:

[Data Source] --> [Strategy Engine] --> [Execution Engine] --> [Broker]

↑↓

[Risk Management] [Monitoring]

7.2. Latency Considerations and Order Execution

Latency is the delay between the moment a trading signal is generated and the order is executed. In strategies like **High -Frequency Trading (HFT)** , minimizing latency is critical.

Sources of Latency:

Data transmission:

Delays in receiving real-time prices from the data provider.

Prosecution:

Time needed to analyze data and generate signals.

Transmission of Orders:

Time to send orders to the broker and receive confirmations.

How to Reduce Latency:

Placement:

Host the system close to the exchange servers to reduce transmission time.

Efficient Infrastructure:

Use high-performance hardware and fast languages like C++ or Java.

Code Optimization:

Minimize unnecessary processes in the strategy logic.

Execution of Orders:

Market Orders:

They guarantee immediate execution at the best available price.

Risk: Exposure to slippage.

Limit Orders:

Execution at the specified price or better.

Risk: Possible non-execution if the market does not reach the price.

Practical Example (Python with Interactive Brokers):

```
from ib_insync import *

# Connect with Interactive Brokers
ib = IB()
ib.connect('127.0.0.1', 7497, clientId=1)

# Configure contract
contract = Stock('AAPL', 'SMART', 'USD')
ib.qualifyContracts(contract)
```

Send a buy order to the market

order = MarketOrder('BUY', 10) # Buy 10 shares

ib.placeOrder(contract, order)

7.3. Risk Management in Algorithmic Trading

Risk management is essential to protecting capital and ensuring the system's sustainability over time. A robust system must include measures to limit losses and diversify exposure.

1. Stop Loss:

A predefined level where the position is automatically closed if the market moves against it.

Example:

Buy shares at $100 with a Stop Loss at $95 to limit losses to $5 per share.

2. Take Profit:

A level at which the position is automatically closed upon reaching the profit target.

Example:

Buy at $100 with a Take Profit at $110 to lock in a profit of $10 per share.

3. Diversification:

Reduce risk by spreading capital across multiple instruments, sectors, or strategies.

Example:

Trade stocks, Forex, and commodities simultaneously to avoid risk concentration.

4. Position Size:

Determine how much capital to allocate to each operation based on the risk level.

Example (1% Rule):

If the total capital is $10,000, risk only $100 (1%) per trade.

5. Daily Loss Limit:

Stop the system if losses exceed a predefined threshold.

Example:

Suspend operations if daily losses reach 5% of capital.

Risk Management Example (MQL5):

```
#include <Trade/Trade.mqh>
CTrade trade;
```

```
// Risk management parameters
input double LotSize = 0.1;
input double StopLoss = 20; // In points
input double TakeProfit = 50; // In points

void OnTick()
{
if (ConditionsForTrade())
{
trade.Buy(LotSize, NULL, Ask, StopLoss, TakeProfit);
}
}
```

Conclusion

Implementing a live trading system requires a robust design, efficient latency management, and a solid risk management strategy. These elements not only optimize trade execution but also protect trader capital from market volatility and uncertainty.

CHAPTER 8

Legal and Regulatory Aspects

Algorithmic trading operates in a highly regulated environment to protect the integrity of financial markets, prevent manipulation, and ensure fair access for all participants. This chapter examines global regulations, the ethical responsibilities of algorithmic traders, and examples of significant legal cases.

8.1. Global Regulations Related to Algorithmic Trading

Regulators around the world have established specific rules to oversee algorithmic trading due to its impact on market stability. These regulations seek to balance technological innovation with the protection of investors and the financial system.

1. Main Areas of Regulation:

Transparency:

It requires algorithmic trading firms to disclose information about their strategies and algorithms to regulatory authorities.

Example: Periodic reports on algorithms used and their impact on the market.

Preventing Market Manipulation:

It prohibits practices such as **spoofing** (placing fake orders to influence the price) and **layering** (creating layers of fake orders to manipulate the market).

Operational Risk Control:

Requirements to ensure that algorithmic systems are secure, reliable, and protected against technical failures.

4. Monitoring and Auditing:

Obligation to maintain detailed records of all transactions and algorithmic activities for future audits.

2. Regulations in Different Jurisdictions:

European Union (MiFID II):

Requires that algorithms be documented and monitored to avoid destabilizing impacts.

It introduces the obligation to carry out stress tests on algorithmic systems.

United States (SEC and CFTC Regulation):

Strict supervision against **spoofing** and high-frequency abuse.

Rule **15c3-5** requires pre-trade risk controls for brokers.

Asia (India and Singapore):

India has implemented regulations limiting the use of co-location and setting higher fees for high-frequency trading.

Singapore requires algorithmic trading firms to demonstrate the robustness of their systems.

8.2. Regulatory Compliance and Ethics Management

Regulatory compliance is not only a legal requirement but also an ethical standard to protect investors and maintain confidence in the markets.

1. Regulatory Compliance:

Internal Supervision:

Companies must implement compliance teams to monitor compliance with regulations.

Conduct regular audits of algorithmic systems.

Testing and Validation:

Before implementing an algorithm, conduct rigorous testing to ensure it complies with legal standards.

Latency Control:

Avoid practices that provide unfair advantages, such as preferential access to market data.

Risk Management:

Implement automatic limits on order size and total exposure to prevent systemic risks.

2. Ethical Management:

Market Impact:

Ensure that algorithmic strategies do not manipulate the market or harm other participants.

Transparency:

Be clear about the risks associated with the use of algorithms in reports to clients or investors.

Social Responsibility:

Design algorithms that promote market stability rather than exploit temporary inefficiencies.

8.3. Examples of Legal Cases in Algorithmic Trading

1. Navinder Sarao Case and the Flash Crash (2010):

Context:

Navinder Sarao was accused of using an algorithm to manipulate the S&P 500 futures market.

spoofing strategy contributed to the "Flash Crash" of May 6, 2010, when the Dow Jones fell nearly 1,000 points in minutes.

Result:

He was extradited to the US and convicted of market manipulation.

2. Citadel Securities Case (2017):

Context:

Citadel was accused of submitting false orders to manipulate the price of certain stocks.

Result:

The SEC fined the company for unfair practices, strengthening oversight of high-frequency algorithms.

3. Barclays and Dark Pools Case (2014):

Context:

Barclays was investigated for misleading investors about algorithmic trading activity in its dark pool.

The algorithms allegedly favored certain high-frequency traders.

Result:

Barclays paid a multi-million-pound fine and faced regulatory restrictions.

4. Post-Flash Crash Regulations:

The 2010 Flash Crash prompted U.S. regulators to implement new rules, such as "limit up-limit down," to prevent sudden price drops.

Conclusion

Algorithmic trading operates under strict regulations designed to ensure integrity and fairness in financial markets. As technologies advance, so do regulations to address emerging risks. Regulatory compliance and ethical management are not only legal obligations but also fundamental pillars for maintaining trust in algorithmic trading systems.

CHAPTER 9

Tools and Resources: Popular Algorithmic Trading Platforms

Algorithmic trading requires a combination of specialized tools and reliable data sources to analyze markets, develop strategies, and execute trades. This chapter covers the most popular platforms, essential data sources, and recommended educational resources for a deeper dive into the topic.

9.1. Popular Algorithmic Trading Platforms

Algorithmic trading platforms provide the necessary environment for designing, testing, and executing automated strategies. Some of the most commonly used ones are highlighted below:

1. MetaTrader (MT4/MT5):

Description:

MetaTrader is a widely used platform for the Forex and CFD markets. It allows for strategy programming using the MQL4 (MT4) and MQL5 (MT5) programming languages.

Characteristics:

Integrated backtesting.

Customizable technical indicators.

Compatible with most retail brokers.

Conditions for Algorithmic Trading :

Programming language : MQL4 (for MT4) and MQL5 (for MT5), specifically designed for building algorithms and customizing indicators.

Backtesting : MT5 offers a multicore strategy tester, allowing simulations with historical data and forward testing.

Markets : Supports forex, stocks, indices, commodities, and cryptocurrencies, depending on the broker used.

Limitations :

MT4 is more limited compared to MT5 in terms of algorithmic trading functionality.

Broker dependence for market data and latency.

Ideal for: Retail traders and beginners in algorithmic trading.

2. NinjaTrader:

Description:

Advanced platform for futures, Forex, and stocks, known for its focus on technical analysis and custom strategy development.

Characteristics:

Own programming language based on C#.

Real-time simulation and advanced backtesting tools.

Conditions for Algorithmic Trading :

Programming language : Uses C#, offering great flexibility and power to build strategies.

Tools : Strategy Builder (graphical interface for non-programmer traders) and NinjaScript (for advanced users).

Backtesting and Simulation : Robust backtesting with detailed analysis tools and real-time simulation.

Markets : Direct support for futures, forex, and stocks, with support for multiple data providers.

Limitations :

Steep learning curve for new users.

Dependence on premium data subscriptions to access real-time data.

Ideal for: Traders looking for programming flexibility and detailed technical analysis.

3. QuantConnect:

Description:

A cloud-based platform that allows you to develop strategies in languages like Python and C#. It offers access to multiple asset classes.

Characteristics:

Access to historical and real-time data.

Integration with brokers such as Interactive Brokers and Alpaca.

Active developer community.

Conditions for Algorithmic Trading :

Supported languages : Python and C#.

Backtesting : Advanced tools with access to over 15 years of historical data.

Infrastructure : Completely cloud-based, eliminating the need for on-premises servers.

Markets : Access to forex, stocks, cryptocurrencies and futures.

Limitations :

Requires basic programming knowledge.

Dependence on your cloud connection to execute strategies.

Ideal for: Traders interested in advanced strategies and machine learning.

4. Interactive Brokers API:

Description:

Robust API that allows you to integrate algorithmic strategies with the Interactive Brokers platform.

Characteristics:

Support for Python, Java, C++, R.

Access to a wide range of financial instruments.

Ideal for: Professional traders who trade multiple assets.

5. Alpaca:

Description:

Cloud-based broker offering a free API for trading US stocks.

Characteristics:

Native support for Python.

No transaction fees.

Paper trading for simulations.

Ideal for: Developers and algorithmic traders looking for simplicity and access to equity markets.

6. TradeStation

Description : TradeStation is a powerful platform for algorithmic traders, with advanced tools for strategy design and execution.

Conditions for Algorithmic Trading :

Programming language : EasyLanguage, designed for trading strategies.

Backtesting : Includes real-time simulation and detailed performance analysis.

Markets : Access to stocks, options, futures and forex.

Integrations : Compatible with external tools for advanced analysis.

Limitations :

Focused on the US market.

Higher commissions compared to other platforms.

7. TWS (Trader Workstation) by Interactive Brokers

Description : TWS is Interactive Brokers' proprietary platform. It offers advanced tools for traders developing automated strategies.

Conditions for Algorithmic Trading :

Supported languages : Python, Java, C++, and more through its advanced API.

Predefined Strategies : Options to implement basic algorithms without coding.

Markets : Access to a wide range of global instruments and markets.

Limitations :

Requires technical expertise to use its API.

Less intuitive interface for beginners.

8. cTrader Automate

Description : cTrader Automate is a C#-based algorithmic trading platform. It offers an alternative to MetaTrader with a more modern approach and advanced tools.

Conditions for Algorithmic Trading :

Programming language : C#, using cTrader API.

Backtesting and Optimization : Integrated tools for evaluating strategies.

Markets : Mainly compatible with forex and CFDs.

Limitations :

Less community and support than MetaTrader.

It depends on the broker for compatibility.

9. MultiCharts

Description : MultiCharts is a platform aimed at technical traders who need advanced analysis and optimization tools.

Conditions for Algorithmic Trading :

Programming language : EasyLanguage and PowerLanguage.

Backtesting and analysis : Robust tools with real-time simulation.

Markets : Compatible with multiple brokers and global markets.

Limitations :

Expensive compared to other platforms.

Steep learning curve.

10. ProRealTime

Description : ProRealTime is a web-based technical analysis and algorithmic trading platform.

Conditions for Algorithmic Trading :

Programming language : ProRealCode, a proprietary language that is easy to learn.

Backtesting : Extensive tools for evaluating strategies with detailed historical data.

Markets : Supports forex, stocks, futures and CFDs.

Limitations :

Based on monthly subscriptions.

Dependence on your cloud connectivity.

11. Zorro Trader

Description : Zorro Trader is a free algorithmic trading tool that supports high-frequency and custom strategies.

Conditions for Algorithmic Trading :

Scripting language : Lightweight and easy to learn.

Backtesting : Advanced functionality with access to historical data.

Markets : Support for forex, stocks and futures.

Limitations :

Less intuitive for beginners.

Requires technical expertise.

9.2. Data Sources

Data is essential for developing and evaluating strategies. The quality, quantity, and frequency of data can determine the success of an algorithmic trading system.

1. Historical Data:

Description:

They allow retrospective analysis and strategy testing under different market conditions.

Common Sources:

Yahoo Finance: Free, with historical data for stocks and currencies.

Quandl: Comprehensive financial, economic and alternative database.

MetaTrader: Integrated data platform for Forex and CFDs.

Uses:

Backtesting and strategy optimization.

2. High Frequency Data:

Description:

Real-time data including prices, volume, and market depth.

Common Sources:

Polygon.io: Real-time data provider for stocks, forex, and cryptocurrencies.

Interactive Brokers: Access real-time data through its API.

Bloomberg Terminal: Premium solution with high-precision data.

Uses:

High-frequency strategies and intraday analysis.

3. Factors to Consider When Choosing a Data Source:

Frequency: Temporality of the data (minute, hour, daily, tick).

Coverage: Available instruments and markets.

Cost: Free fonts vs. premium solutions.

Quality: Data accuracy and consistency.

9.3. Recommended Books and Courses for Deeper Learning in Algorithmic Trading

Recommended Books:

"Algorithmic Trading: Winning Strategies and Their Rationale" – Ernie Chan

Explore profitable strategies and the practical implementation of algorithmic systems.

"Quantitative Trading: How to Build Your Own Algorithmic Trading Business" – Ernie Chan

Detailed introduction to quantitative strategy design.

"Advances in Financial Machine Learning" – Marcos López de Prado

Covers advanced machine learning techniques applied to trading.

"Python for Algorithmic Trading" – Yves Hilpisch

Practical use of Python to develop algorithmic trading strategies.

"Trading and Exchanges: Market Microstructure for Practitioners" – Larry Harris

Delve into market microstructure and its impact on trading.

Recommended Courses:

"Algorithmic Trading and Finance Models with Python, R, and Stata Essential Training" (LinkedIn Learning):

Introductory course that combines theory and practice with examples in Python and R.

"Machine Learning for Trading" (Udacity):

Advanced course that combines machine learning with quantitative finance.

"AlgoTrading101 by Quantra" (QuantInsti):

Practical course designed for traders who want to learn the fundamentals of algorithmic trading.

"Quantitative Finance Specialization" (Coursera):

Focused on quantitative strategies and financial modeling.

"Interactive Brokers API Workshop" (Interactive Brokers):

Specific course to learn how to integrate strategies with the IBKR API.

Conclusion

Success in algorithmic trading depends on access to the right tools, data, and knowledge. Platforms like MetaTrader and QuantConnect provide accessible environments for developing strategies, while data sources like Quandl and Polygon.io offer the insights needed to analyze them. Finally, recommended books and courses allow you to delve deeper into the technical and practical aspects of algorithmic trading, from the basics to advanced techniques.

CHAPTER 10

ALGORITHMIC TRADING PROGRAMMING BUILDER

Some Programming Builders for Algorithmic Trading

EA Builder: Graphical tool for MetaTrader. **Forex Strategy Builder**: Ideal for beginners. **StrategyQuant**: Automatic strategy generator.

Here's a list of algorithmic trading software builders, along with a description of each:

10.1. EA Builder

EA Builder is an algorithm creation tool designed for traders who want to develop automated strategies without advanced programming knowledge. It's designed for creating Expert Advisors (EAs) for platforms such as MetaTrader 4 (MT4) and MetaTrader 5 (MT5).

Main features :

Intuitive graphical interface.

Automatic generation of MQL4/MQL5 code.

Supports custom indicators.

Allows you to create strategies based on technical indicators and user-defined rules.

Advantages :

Ideal for beginners.

No programming knowledge required.

It offers a free version with basic functions.

Limitations :

Limited options in the free version.

Not suitable for extremely complex strategies.

10.2. Forex Strategy Builder (FSB)

Forex Strategy Builder is a software program specialized in creating and testing strategies for the forex market. It allows you to develop strategies using a visual interface and perform backtesting to evaluate their performance.

Main features :

It allows you to build strategies based on predefined indicators and rules.

Detailed backtesting with performance analysis.

Compatible with MetaTrader 4 and 5.

Includes an automatic strategy generator.

Advantages :

Wide options to optimize strategies.

Advanced simulation tools.

Ideal for forex-focused traders.

Limitations :

Less compatible with other markets outside of forex.

10.3. StrategyQuant

StrategyQuant is an advanced tool that uses artificial intelligence and machine learning to generate algorithmic trading strategies. It's ideal for traders looking for a more automated approach to strategy design.

Main features :

Automatic generation of strategies based on historical data.

Support for multiple markets: forex, stocks, futures, etc.

Optimization and validation with out-of-sample data.

Export strategies to MetaTrader, NinjaTrader and other platforms.

Advantages :

Advanced analysis and optimization tools.

It allows you to create innovative strategies without the need for programming.

Extensive technical support and active community.

Limitations :

Expensive compared to other builders.

Steeper learning curve.

10.4. AlgoWizard (Quantower)

AlgoWizard is a Quantower tool that allows you to build trading strategies using visual blocks, without writing code. It's designed for traders who want a quick and easy solution for developing strategies.

Main features :

Building strategies through a system of visual blocks.

Integration with multiple brokers and platforms.

Integrated backtesting and optimization tools.

Supports real-time data.

Advantages :

Clean and easy to use interface.

Compatible with multiple markets and assets.

Support for both simple and complex strategies.

Limitations :

Requires connection to compatible brokers.

Less customizable compared to manual development.

10.5. VisualTrader

VisualTrader is a software that combines technical analysis and strategy building in a visual environment. Its main focus is helping traders identify opportunities and automate strategies without programming.

Main features :

Creating strategies based on price patterns and technical indicators.

Integration with trading platforms such as MetaTrader and TradeStation.

Advanced analysis and risk management tools.

Advantages :

Strong focus on technical analysis.

Ideal for visual and technical traders.

Compatible with multiple platforms.

Limitations :

It may be limiting for strategies based on fundamentalist data.

10.6. Zorro Trader

Zorro Trader is a lightweight, free tool that allows you to develop algorithmic trading strategies using a simple scripting language. It is designed for advanced traders and developers.

Main features :

Easy-to-learn scripting language.

Compatible with multiple broker platforms and APIs.

Ideal for customized strategies.

Support for high-frequency trading (HFT).

Advantages :

Free and open source software.

Ideal for technical traders with some programming experience.

High flexibility and customization.

Limitations :

Learning curve for beginners.

Less intuitive than other graphic-based builders.

10.7. QuantConnect

QuantConnect is a cloud-based platform that allows you to develop, test, and execute algorithmic strategies across multiple markets. Although it's not a traditional builder, it offers a user-friendly environment for creating algorithms.

Main features :

Compatible with languages such as Python and C#.

Extensive library of historical data for backtesting.

Connection with multiple brokers.

Active community to share ideas and strategies.

Advantages :

Access to massive amounts of data and powerful backtesting tools.

Ideal for advanced and quantitative traders.

Scalable for complex strategies.

Limitations :

Requires basic programming knowledge.

Dependence on internet connection due to its cloud-based focus.

10.8. NinjaTrader Strategy Builder

NinjaTrader's Strategy Builder allows traders to design automated strategies using a graphical interface. It's an excellent option for traders using the NinjaTrader platform.

Main features :

Graphical interface to build strategies without code.

Native integration with the NinjaTrader platform.

Advanced backtesting and optimization tools.

Advantages :

Perfect for NinjaTrader users.

Advanced risk analysis and management options.

Support for futures, forex, and stocks.

Limitations :

Limited to NinjaTrader users.

Less flexible than manual development in C#.

10.9. Tradestation Strategy Builder

TradeStation's strategy builder uses its proprietary EasyLanguage to make it easy to create algorithmic trading strategies.

Main features :

Easy integration with the TradeStation platform.

Support for strategies based on technical indicators.

Advanced performance analysis.

Advantages :

Ideal for traders operating on TradeStation.

Intuitive interface for beginners.

Limitations :

Limited to TradeStation platform.

These builders offer a wide range of options for traders of all levels, from beginners to experts. Depending on your needs and experience level, you can choose the one that best suits your trading goals.

CHAPTER 11

VPS FOR HOSTING AND CONTINUOUS OPERATION

A VPS allows you to run algorithms 24/7. Popular providers include: Amazon AWS, Google Cloud, Vultr, and MetaTrader VPS.

Below is a list of Virtual Private Server (VPS) providers suitable for algorithmic trading, detailing their features, suitability for trading types, pricing, and their relationship with specific brokers or platforms:

11.1. Beeks Financial Cloud

Description : Specialized provider of VPS solutions for the financial sector, offering low latency and high reliability.

Characteristics :

Locations : Data centers in proximity to major global stock exchanges, including New York, London, and Tokyo.

Latency : Optimized for high-frequency trading (HFT) and time-sensitive strategies.

Security : Robust measures to protect data and operations.

Suitability : Ideal for professional traders and HFT strategies that require fast and stable execution.

Price : Plans start at approximately $30 USD per month, varying based on selected resources and locations.

Partnerships : Works with brokers like BlackBull Markets, offering integrated VPS services for their clients. cite turn0search3

11.2. MetaTrader VPS

Description : VPS hosting service integrated directly into the MetaTrader 4 and 5 platforms, facilitating the continuous execution of Expert Advisors (EAs) .

Characteristics :

Integration : Easy configuration from the MetaTrader platform.

Latency : Low, due to proximity to MetaTrader servers.

Availability : 99.9% uptime guaranteed.

Suitability : Suitable for traders using EAs in MetaTrader and looking for an integrated and easy-to-configure solution.

Price : Approximately $15 USD per month, with variations depending on the broker and region.

Partnerships : Available for MetaTrader users through supported brokers. citeturn0search10

11.3. ForexVPS

Description : VPS provider focused on forex traders, offering servers optimized for popular trading platforms.

Characteristics :

Optimization : Servers specifically configured for MetaTrader and cTrader.

Latency : ☐Low, with servers located near major financial centers. ☐

Support : 24/7 specialized in trading.

Suitability : ☐Ideal for forex traders who require an optimized VPS solution for their trading platforms.☐

Price : ☐Plans start at $25 USD per month, with more advanced options available. ☐

Partnerships : ☐It is not affiliated with any specific broker, but is compatible with most trading platforms.☐

11.4. AxiTrader VPS

Description : ☐Broker that offers free VPS services to its clients who meet certain trading volume criteria. ☐

Characteristics :

Integration : ☐Direct with AxiTrader trading accounts.☐

Latency : ☐Low, optimized for AxiTrader servers.☐

Cost : ☐Free for clients who maintain a specific trading volume. ☐

Suitability : Beneficial for AxiTrader clients looking to reduce costs and improve the execution of their algorithmic strategies.

Price : Free under conditions; otherwise, standard rates apply.

Associations : Exclusive service for AxiTrader clients. citeturn0search6

11.5. Amazon Web Services (AWS) - EC2

Description : Leading cloud services provider, offering virtual server instances with high flexibility and scalability.

Characteristics :

Flexibility : Wide range of hardware configurations and geographic locations.

Scalability : Ability to adjust resources according to the trader's needs.

Security : Robust infrastructure with advanced security measures.

Suitability : Suitable for technically savvy traders who require customization and scalability in their operations.

Price : Varies by configuration; options start at $10 USD per month for basic instances.

Partnerships : ☐Not associated with any specific broker or platform; requires manual configuration to integrate trading platforms. ☐

11.6. Google Cloud Platform (GCP) - Compute Engine

Description : ☐Google cloud computing service, offering virtual machines with high availability and performance. ☐

Characteristics :

Performance : ☐High-speed servers with SSD storage options. ☐

Network : ☐Low-latency global network infrastructure. ☐

Scalability : ☐Dynamic adjustment of resources based on demand. ☐

Suitability : ☐Ideal for traders looking for a robust and scalable infrastructure, with experience in server configuration. ☐

Pricing : Pay-as-you-go models; basic instances start at $15 USD per month.

Partnerships : ☐Not associated with brokers ; requires configuration to integrate trading platforms. ☐

11.7. Microsoft Azure - Virtual Machines

Description : Microsoft's cloud computing platform , offering virtual machines with various configurations and complementary services.

Characteristics :

Integration : ☐Compatibility with Microsoft tools and services.☐

Security : ☐Compliance with international security and privacy standards . ☐

COMPARATIVE CHART

Supplier	Description	Suitability	Price (USD/month)	Association
Beeks Financial Cloud	Specialized in financial solutions, low latency.	HFT and professional trading.	From $30	Collaborate with brokers like BlackBull Markets.
MetaTrader VPS	Integrated directly into MetaTrader 4 and 5.	EAs in MetaTrader.	From $15	Exclusive for MetaTrader.
Forex VPS	Optimized for popular trading platforms.	Optimized Forex trading.	From $25	Compatible with most brokers.
AxiTrader VPS	Free for customers who meet	AxiTrader clients	Free under conditi	Exclusive service

	volume criteria.	with frequent trading.	ons	of AxiTrader.
Amazon Web Services (AWS)	Flexibility and scalability in the cloud.	Traders with personalized needs.	From $10	Not associated with brokers.
Google Cloud Platform (GCP)	High-performance virtual machines.	Advanced and technical traders.	From $15	Not associated with brokers.

CHAPTER 12

Future Perspectives

12.1. Artificial intelligence and the future of trading

The integration of artificial intelligence (AI) into algorithmic trading is radically transforming the way trades are analyzed and executed in the financial markets. Advances in machine learning allow algorithms to identify complex patterns in historical and real-time data, providing a significant advantage in anticipating market movements.

Current and future applications of AI in trading include:

Advanced Predictive Systems : AI models can predict price trends, identify buy/sell signals, and dynamically adjust strategies.

Natural Language Processing (NLP) : Tools that analyze news, social media, and other content to assess market sentiment and its potential impact.

Adaptive Trading : Algorithms that automatically adjust strategies based on sudden changes in volatility or liquidity.

Evolution towards virtual financial assistants : Platforms that not only execute transactions but also offer personalized advice in real time.

The future of AI-powered algorithmic trading suggests greater access to sophisticated tools for retail traders, as well as more intense competition in financial markets. However, this also raises ethical and regulatory challenges, such as transparency in algorithms and the potential risks of over-automation.

12.2. Blockchain and Decentralized Algorithmic Trading

Blockchain technology is revolutionizing not only finance but also algorithmic trading. The concept of decentralized trading (DeFi trading) eliminates intermediaries such as banks and brokers, allowing for the direct execution of trades on blockchain platforms through smart contracts.

Advantages of blockchain-based algorithmic trading:

Transparency : All transactions and strategies executed through blockchain are publicly accessible, ensuring trust and eliminating unfair practices.

Security : Smart contracts are immutable and automated, minimizing the risk of manipulation.

Global Access : Allows anyone with an Internet connection to participate in decentralized markets.

Asset Tokenization : The ability to create and trade digital assets backed by real-world securities, such as stocks, bonds, or commodities.

However, the integration of blockchain into algorithmic trading faces challenges such as scalability, the volatility of cryptocurrencies, and the need for clear regulation to protect investors.

12.3. Challenges and Opportunities in Emerging Markets

Emerging markets represent fertile ground for the development and expansion of algorithmic trading due to factors such as rapid digitalization, economic growth, and the adoption of new technologies. However, they also present unique challenges that differentiate them from developed markets.

Opportunities:

Developing infrastructure : New digital financial platforms and markets in emerging countries allow for the straightforward implementation of modern algorithmic trading systems.

Higher potential returns : Volatility and economic growth offer opportunities for algorithmic strategies that take advantage of significant price movements.

Democratizing Access : Access to algorithmic trading tools can attract retail investors in markets with high demand for financial inclusion.

Challenges:

Regulatory limitations : Many emerging markets lack adequate legal frameworks for the operation of complex algorithms.

Insufficient or low-quality data : Algorithms depend on reliable and consistent data, which can be a problem in these markets.

Uneven technological infrastructure : Limited connectivity and high costs of accessing platforms can restrict mass adoption.

Overcoming these challenges requires close collaboration between governments, financial institutions, and technology developers. It also offers an opportunity for emerging markets to become leaders in financial innovation in the near future.

These concepts complement the analysis of the current algorithmic trading landscape, focusing on its projections and strategic challenges for the future.

ANNEXES

Basic code example in MQL5 for opening and closing positions.

Here's an example of an MQL5 **Expert Advisor (EA)** that opens positions based on the intersection of two moving averages: one 8-period and the other 22-period. This EA will open buy positions when the 8-period moving average crosses above the 22-period moving average, and sell positions when the 8-period moving average crosses below the 22-period moving average. It also includes a trailing stop, stop loss, and take profit.

EA Code

```
//+------------------------------------------------------------+
//| EA based on moving averages |
//+------------------------------------------------------------+
#property copyright "EA based on moving averages"
#property version "1.00"
#property strict
```

// Input parameters

input int FastPeriod = 8; // Period of the fast average

input int SlowPeriod = 22; // Slow average period

input double LotSize = 0.1; // Lot size

input double TakeProfit = 50; // Take Profit in points

input double StopLoss = 50; // Stop Loss in points

input double TrailingStop = 20; // Trailing Stop in points

// Global variables

double FastMA, SlowMA, PrevFastMA, PrevSlowMA;

//+--+
//| Expert initialization function |
//+--+
int OnInit()
{

```
Print("EA initialized. Operating with averages of ", FastPeriod, " and ", SlowPeriod);
return(INIT_SUCCEEDED);
}


//+------------------------------------------------------------+
//| Expert deinitialization function |
//+------------------------------------------------------------+
void OnDeinit(const int reason)
{
Print("EA stopped.");
}


//+------------------------------------------------------------+
//| Expert tick function |
//+------------------------------------------------------------+
void OnTick()
{
// Calculation of moving averages
```

```
FastMA = iMA(NULL, 0, FastPeriod, 0, MODE_EMA, PRICE_CLOSE, 0);

SlowMA = iMA(NULL, 0, SlowPeriod, 0, MODE_EMA, PRICE_CLOSE, 0);

PrevFastMA = iMA(NULL, 0, FastPeriod, 0, MODE_EMA, PRICE_CLOSE, 1);

PrevSlowMA = iMA(NULL, 0, SlowPeriod, 0, MODE_EMA, PRICE_CLOSE, 1);


// Trailing stop management
ManageTrailingStop();


// Crosschecking
if (PrevFastMA < PrevSlowMA && FastMA > SlowMA) // Cross up
{
OpenBuy();
}
else if (PrevFastMA > PrevSlowMA && FastMA < SlowMA) // Cross Down
{
OpenSell();
}
}
```

//+--+

//| Function to open buy positions |

//+--+

void OpenBuy()

{

if (PositionsTotal() == 0)

{

double ask = SymbolInfoDouble(_Symbol, SYMBOL_ASK);

double sl = ask - StopLoss * _Point;

double tp = ask + TakeProfit * _Point;

int ticket = OrderSend(_Symbol, OP_BUY, LotSize, ask, 2, sl, tp, "Purchase by crossing", 0, 0, clrGreen);

if (ticket < 0)

Print("Error opening purchase: ", GetLastError());

else

Print("Purchase open: ", ticket);

}

}

//+--+
//| Function to open sell positions |
//+--+
```
void OpenSell()
{
if (PositionsTotal() == 0)
{
double bid = SymbolInfoDouble(_Symbol, SYMBOL_BID);
double sl = bid + StopLoss * _Point;
double tp = bid - TakeProfit * _Point;
int ticket = OrderSend(_Symbol, OP_SELL, LotSize, bid, 2, sl, tp, "Sale by crossing", 0, 0, clrRed);
if (ticket < 0)
Print("Error opening sale: ", GetLastError());
else
Print("Open sale: ", ticket);
}
}
```

//+--+
//| Function to manage the Trailing Stop |
//+--+
void ManageTrailingStop()
{
for (int i = 0; i < PositionsTotal(); i++)
{
ulong ticket = PositionGetTicket(i);
double price = PositionGetDouble(POSITION_PRICE_OPEN);
double sl = PositionGetDouble(POSITION_SL);
double tp = PositionGetDouble(POSITION_TP);
double currentPrice = (PositionGetInteger(POSITION_TYPE) == POSITION_TYPE_BUY) ? SymbolInfoDouble(_Symbol, SYMBOL_BID) : SymbolInfoDouble(_Symbol, SYMBOL_ASK);

if (PositionGetInteger(POSITION_TYPE) == POSITION_TYPE_BUY)

```
{
    double newSL = currentPrice - TrailingStop * _Point;
    if (newSL > sl)
    {
        if (!OrderModify(ticket, price, newSL, tp, 0))
            Print("Error modifying purchase SL: ", GetLastError());
    }
}
else if (PositionGetInteger(POSITION_TYPE) == POSITION_TYPE_SELL)
{
    double newSL = currentPrice + TrailingStop * _Point;
    if (newSL < sl)
    {
        if (!OrderModify(ticket, price, newSL, tp, 0))
            Print("Error modifying SL of sale: ", GetLastError());
    }
}
}
```

EA Features:

Conditions for opening positions:

Buy: Upward crossing of the 8 EMA over the 22 EMA.

Sell: Downward crossing of the 8 EMA over the 22 EMA.

Stop Loss and Take Profit:

Configurable at points through input parameters.

Trailing Stop:

Dynamically adjusts the Stop Loss level to protect profits.

Control of open positions:

Ensures that only one position is open at a time.

Settings:

You can modify the FastPeriod and SlowPeriod values to change the periods of the moving averages.

Adjust the TakeProfit, StopLoss, and TrailingStop values according to your strategy.

Below I detail each of the sections of this code:

1. Declaration of Properties and Input Parameters

#property copyright "EA based on moving averages"

#property version "1.00"

#property strict

input int FastPeriod = 8; // Period of the fast average

input int SlowPeriod = 22; // Slow average period

input double LotSize = 0.1; // Lot size

input double TakeProfit = 50; // Take Profit in points

input double StopLoss = 50; // Stop Loss in points

input double TrailingStop = 20; // Trailing Stop in points

Properties: Specify program information such as copyright, version, and strict coding style to avoid common errors.

Input parameters : Allow you to customize the EA values without having to modify the code:

FastPeriod and SlowPeriod: Determine the periods of the fast and slow moving averages.

LotSize: Lot size for operations.

TakeProfit and StopLoss: Set profit and loss levels.

TrailingStop: Defines the distance (in points) to dynamically adjust the Stop Loss.

2. Global Variables

double FastMA, SlowMA, PrevFastMA, PrevSlowMA;

These variables store the current and previous values of the fast and slow moving averages. They are used to identify crossovers.

3. OnInit Function

```
int OnInit()
{
Print("EA initialized. Operating with averages of ", FastPeriod, " and ", SlowPeriod);
return(INIT_SUCCEEDED);
}
```

Purpose: Initializes the EA when it is loaded onto the chart.

Action: Print a message to the log to confirm that the EA has been loaded successfully.

4. OnDeinit Function

void OnDeinit(const int reason)

{

Print("EA stopped.");

}

Purpose: Executes actions when the EA is removed from the chart.

Action: Print a message indicating that the EA has been stopped.

5. OnTick Function

void OnTick()

{

// Calculation of moving averages

FastMA = iMA(NULL, 0, FastPeriod, 0, MODE_EMA, PRICE_CLOSE, 0);

SlowMA = iMA(NULL, 0, SlowPeriod, 0, MODE_EMA, PRICE_CLOSE, 0);

PrevFastMA = iMA(NULL, 0, FastPeriod, 0, MODE_EMA, PRICE_CLOSE, 1);

```
PrevSlowMA = iMA(NULL, 0, SlowPeriod, 0,
MODE_EMA, PRICE_CLOSE, 1);


// Trailing stop management
ManageTrailingStop();


// Crosschecking
if (PrevFastMA < PrevSlowMA && FastMA > SlowMA) // Cross up
{
OpenBuy();
}
else if (PrevFastMA > PrevSlowMA && FastMA < SlowMA) // Cross Down
{
OpenSell();
}
}
```

Purpose: Executes the EA's main actions every time there is a new price *tick* .

Actions:

Moving Average Calculation : Obtains the current and previous values of the fast and slow moving averages using the iMA function.

Manage Trailing Stop : Call the ManageTrailingStop function to dynamically adjust the Stop Loss.

Checking crosses :

If the fast average crosses upward over the slow average, call OpenBuy.

If it crosses to the downside, call OpenSell.

---

6. OpenBuy Function

void OpenBuy()

{

if (PositionsTotal() == 0)

{

double ask = SymbolInfoDouble(_Symbol, SYMBOL_ASK);

double sl = ask - StopLoss * _Point;

double tp = ask + TakeProfit * _Point;

int ticket = OrderSend(_Symbol, OP_BUY, LotSize, ask, 2, sl, tp, "Purchase by cross", 0, 0, clrGreen);

if (ticket < 0)

Print("Error opening purchase: ", GetLastError());

else

Print("Purchase open: ", ticket);

}

}

Purpose: Open a buy position if there are no open positions.

Actions:

Check that there are no open positions (PositionsTotal).

Calculates entry, stop loss and take profit prices.

Use OrderSend to send a purchase order.

Prints a message confirming the operation or indicating an error.

---

7. OpenSell Function

void OpenSell()

{

if (PositionsTotal() == 0)

{

double bid = SymbolInfoDouble(_Symbol, SYMBOL_BID);

double sl = bid + StopLoss * _Point;

double tp = bid - TakeProfit * _Point;

```
int ticket = OrderSend(_Symbol, OP_SELL, LotSize, bid, 2, sl, tp, "Sale by crossing", 0, 0, clrRed);
if (ticket < 0)
Print("Error opening sale: ", GetLastError());
else
Print("Open sale: ", ticket);
}
}
```

Purpose: Opens a sell position if there are no open positions.

Actions: Similar to OpenBuy, but adjusts prices for a sale transaction.

---

8. ManageTrailingStop Function

```
void ManageTrailingStop()
{
for (int i = 0; i < PositionsTotal(); i++)
{
ulong ticket = PositionGetTicket(i);
double price = PositionGetDouble(POSITION_PRICE_OPEN);
```

```
double sl = PositionGetDouble(POSITION_SL);
double tp = PositionGetDouble(POSITION_TP);
double currentPrice = (PositionGetInteger(POSITION_TYPE) == POSITION_TYPE_BUY) ? SymbolInfoDouble(_Symbol, SYMBOL_BID) : SymbolInfoDouble(_Symbol, SYMBOL_ASK);

if (PositionGetInteger(POSITION_TYPE) == POSITION_TYPE_BUY)
{
double newSL = currentPrice - TrailingStop * _Point;
if (newSL > sl)
{
if (!OrderModify(ticket, price, newSL, tp, 0))
Print("Error modifying purchase SL: ", GetLastError());
}
}
else if (PositionGetInteger(POSITION_TYPE) == POSITION_TYPE_SELL)
```

```
{
    double newSL = currentPrice + TrailingStop * _Point;
    if (newSL < sl)
    {
        if (!OrderModify(ticket, price, newSL, tp, 0))
            Print("Error modifying SL of sale: ", GetLastError());
    }
   }
  }
 }
}
```

Purpose: Dynamically adjusts Stop Loss to protect profits when price moves in your favor.

Actions:

It goes through all open positions.

Calculates a new Stop Loss level based on the current price.

Update the Stop Loss if the new level is more favorable.

Glossary of Key MQL5 Terms

EA (Expert Advisor) : An automated program that operates in the financial markets according to rules defined by the user.

Indicator : Tool that analyzes price and volume data to generate trading signals.

Symbol : A financial instrument, such as a currency pair (e.g., EUR/USD) or an asset (e.g., stocks, indices).

Timeframe : Time interval for each candle or bar (eg, M1, H1, D1).

OrderSend : Function that sends orders to the market (buy or sell).

OrderModify : Modifies an existing order, such as adjusting the Stop Loss or Take Profit.

OrderClose : Closes an open position.

Stop Loss (SL) : Predetermined level where a position will be closed to limit losses.

Take Profit (TP) : Predetermined level where a position will be closed to lock in profits.

Trailing Stop : Dynamic Stop Loss that adjusts automatically to protect profits.

iMA (Moving Average) : Built-in function for calculating moving averages.

iRSI (Relative Strength Index) : Built-in function to calculate the relative strength index.

MODE_MAIN : Constant that indicates the main value of a technical indicator.

PositionGetDouble : Retrieves open position data, such as entry prices or SL.

PositionsTotal() : Returns the total number of open positions.

SymbolInfoDouble() : Retrieves information about a symbol, such as opening price or tick size.

OnInit() : Function that is executed when the EA or indicator is started.

OnDeinit() : Function that is executed when the EA or indicator is deactivated.

OnTick() : Function that is executed every time a new tick (price change) arrives.

ENUM_TIMEFRAMES : Enumeration that defines the time frames (e.g., PERIOD_M1, PERIOD_H1).

ENUM_ORDER_TYPE : Enumeration of order types, such as OP_BUY or OP_SELL.

Basic Python code example for opening and closing positions.

Python script that implements trading logic based on 8- and 22-period moving averages, using the **MetaTrader5 library** (MetaTrader5 must be installed for the script to work).

The script will execute buy trades when the fast moving average (8 periods) crosses upwards through the slow moving average (22 periods) and sell trades when the fast moving average crosses downwards through the slow moving average. It also includes logic for stop losses, take profits, and trailing stops.

Python code

import MetaTrader5 as MT5

import time

Script parameters

SYMBOL = "EURUSD" # Symbol to trade

LOT_SIZE = 0.1 # Batch size

FAST_PERIOD = 8 # Period of the fast average

SLOW_PERIOD = 22 # Period of the slow average

```python
TAKE_PROFIT = 50 # Take Profit in points
STOP_LOSS = 50 # Stop Loss in points
TRAILING_STOP = 20 # Trailing Stop in points
TIMEFRAME = mt5.TIMEFRAME_M1 # Timeframe (1 minute)

# Connecting to MetaTrader 5
if not mt5.initialize():
    print("Error initializing MetaTrader 5")
    quit()


def get_moving_averages(symbol, timeframe, fast_period, slow_period):
    """
    Calculate fast and slow moving averages.
    """
    rates = mt5.copy_rates_from_pos(symbol, timeframe, 0, slow_period + 1)
    if rates is None or len(rates) < slow_period:
        return None, None

    closes = [rate['close'] for rate in rates]
```

```
fast_ma = sum(closes[-fast_period:]) / fast_period
slow_ma = sum(closes[-slow_period:]) / slow_period
return fast_ma, slow_ma


def open_position(symbol, action, lot_size, stop_loss, take_profit):
    """
    Open a buy or sell position.
    """
    price = mt5.symbol_info_tick(symbol).ask if action == "buy" else mt5.symbol_info_tick(symbol).bid
    point = mt5.symbol_info(symbol).point

    sl = price - stop_loss * point if action == "buy" else price + stop_loss * point
    tp = price + take_profit * point if action == "buy" else price - take_profit * point

    request = {
        "action": mt5.TRADE_ACTION_DEAL,
        "symbol": symbol,
```

```python
"volume": lot_size,
"type": mt5.ORDER_TYPE_BUY if action ==
"buy" else mt5.ORDER_TYPE_SELL,
"price": price,
"sl": sl,
"tp": tp,
"deviation": 20,
"magic": 123456,
"comment": "Trade by script",
}

result = mt5.order_send(request)
if result.retcode != mt5.TRADE_RETCODE_DONE:
    print(f"Error opening position: {result.comment}")
else:
    print(f"Position opened successfully: {result.order}")

def manage_trailing_stop():
    """
    Manages the trailing stop for all open positions.
    """
```

```
positions = mt5.positions_get(symbol=SYMBOL)
if positions is None:
    print("Error getting positions")
    return

for position in positions:
    price = position.price_open
    current_price = mt5.symbol_info_tick(SYMBOL).bid if position.type == mt5.ORDER_TYPE_BUY else mt5.symbol_info_tick(SYMBOL).ask
    sl = position.sl
    point = mt5.symbol_info(SYMBOL).point

    if position.type == mt5.ORDER_TYPE_BUY:
        new_sl = current_price - TRAILING_STOP * point
        if new_sl > sl:
            modify_stop_loss(position.ticket, new_sl)
    elif position.type == mt5.ORDER_TYPE_SELL:
        new_sl = current_price + TRAILING_STOP * point
```

```python
if new_sl < sl:
    modify_stop_loss(position.ticket, new_sl)

def modify_stop_loss(ticket, new_sl):
    """
    Modify the Stop Loss of a position.
    """
    request = {
        "action": mt5.TRADE_ACTION_SLTP,
        "position": ticket,
        "sl": new_sl,
        "tp": None,
    }

    result = mt5.order_send(request)
    if result.retcode != mt5.TRADE_RETCODE_DONE:
        print(f"Error modifying Stop Loss: {result.comment}")
    else:
        print(f"Stop Loss updated: {result.order}")

# Main loop
```

```
try:
    print("Starting the trading script...")
    while True:
        fast_ma, slow_ma = get_moving_averages(SYMBOL, TIMEFRAME, FAST_PERIOD, SLOW_PERIOD)
        if fast_ma is None or slow_ma is None:
            print("Waiting for sufficient data...")
            time.sleep(10)
            continue

        positions = mt5.positions_total()

        if fast_ma > slow_ma:
            # Bullish Crossover
            if positions == 0:  # Check that there are no open positions
                open_position(SYMBOL, "buy", LOT_SIZE, STOP_LOSS, TAKE_PROFIT)
        elif fast_ma < slow_ma:
            # Downward crossing
            if positions == 0:  # Check that there are no open positions
```

```
open_position(SYMBOL, "sell", LOT_SIZE, STOP_LOSS, TAKE_PROFIT)

# Manage trailing stop
manage_trailing_stop()

time.sleep(10)  # Wait 10 seconds before checking again

except KeyboardInterrupt:
    print("Script stopped manually.")
finally:
    mt5.shutdown()
```

Explanation of the Code:

Getting Moving Averages : The get_moving_averages function is used to calculate fast and slow moving averages using closing prices.

Position Opening : The open_position function opens buy or sell trades with the calculated Stop Loss and Take Profit values.

Trailing Stop Management : manage_trailing_stop dynamically updates the Stop Loss to protect profits.

Main Cycle : Checks every 10 seconds if the average crossover conditions are met and executes the corresponding actions.

Requirements:

MetaTrader 5 : Must be installed and configured.

MetaTrader5 Library : Installable with pip install MetaTrader5.

Active Symbol : Make sure the symbol (e.g., EURUSD) is available in your account.

Below, I'll explain what each section of the **Python script** for algorithmic trading determines:

---

1. Script Parameters

SYMBOL = "EURUSD" # Symbol to trade

LOT_SIZE = 0.1 # Batch size

FAST_PERIOD = 8 # Period of the fast average

SLOW_PERIOD = 22 # Period of the slow average

TAKE_PROFIT – 50 # Take Profit in points

STOP_LOSS = 50 # Stop Loss in points

TRAILING_STOP = 20 # Trailing Stop in points

TIMEFRAME = mt5.TIMEFRAME_M1 # Timeframe (1 minute)

Definition : These are the configurable parameters that control the logic of the script.

SYMBOL : The currency pair or asset the script will trade on.

LOT_SIZE : Lot size for each operation.

FAST_PERIOD and SLOW_PERIOD : Periods of the fast and slow moving averages.

TAKE_PROFIT and STOP_LOSS : Profit and loss levels in points.

TRAILING_STOP : Distance in points for the Trailing Stop.

TIMEFRAME : Timeframe used to analyze the data.

---

2. Connecting to MetaTrader 5

if not mt5.initialize():

print("Error initializing MetaTrader 5")

quit()

Definition : This block initializes the connection to the MetaTrader 5 platform.

If it cannot connect, it displays an error message and stops the script.

MetaTrader 5 must be installed and configured correctly.

---

3. get_moving_averages function

def get_moving_averages(symbol, timeframe, fast_period, slow_period):

rates = mt5.copy_rates_from_pos(symbol, timeframe, 0, slow_period + 1)

if rates is None or len(rates) < slow_period:

return None, None

closes = [rate['close'] for rate in rates]

fast_ma = sum(closes[-fast_period:]) / fast_period

slow_ma = sum(closes[-slow_period:]) / slow_period

return fast_ma, slow_ma

Definition : Calculates fast and slow moving averages based on closing prices.

Tickets :

symbol: The asset.

timeframe: The timeframe (e.g., 1 minute).

fast_period and slow_period: The periods of the moving averages.

Outputs : Returns the values of the fast and slow moving averages.

Use mt5.copy_rates_from_pos to get historical data.

---

4. open_position function

def open_position(symbol, action, lot_size, stop_loss, take_profit):

price = mt5.symbol_info_tick(symbol).ask if action == "buy" else mt5.symbol_info_tick(symbol).bid

point = mt5.symbol_info(symbol).point

sl = price - stop_loss * point if action == "buy" else price + stop_loss * point

tp = price + take_profit * point if action == "buy" else price - take_profit * point

request = {

"action": mt5.TRADE_ACTION_DEAL,

"symbol": symbol,

"volume": lot_size,

```
"type": mt5.ORDER_TYPE_BUY if action ==
"buy" else mt5.ORDER_TYPE_SELL,
"price": price,
"sl": sl,
"tp": tp,
"deviation": 20,
"magic": 123456,
"comment": "Trade by script",
}


result = mt5.order_send(request)
if result.retcode !=
mt5.TRADE_RETCODE_DONE:
print(f"Error opening position:
{result.comment}")
else:
print(f"Position opened successfully:
{result.order}")
```

Definition : Open a buy or sell position.

Tickets :

symbol: Active.

action: Type of operation ("buy" or "sell").

lot_size: Batch size.

stop_loss and take_profit: Distances in points for SL and TP.

Actions :

Calculate entry, SL and TP prices.

Send a trade request to MetaTrader 5 with mt5.order_send.

Check the result of the operation and print a message.

---

5. manage_trailing_stop function

def manage_trailing_stop():

positions = mt5.positions_get(symbol=SYMBOL)

if positions is None:

print("Error getting positions")

return

for position in positions:

price = position.price_open

current_price = mt5.symbol_info_tick(SYMBOL).bid if position.type == mt5.ORDER_TYPE_BUY else mt5.symbol_info_tick(SYMBOL).ask

sl = position.sl

```
point = mt5.symbol_info(SYMBOL).point

if position.type == mt5.ORDER_TYPE_BUY:
    new_sl = current_price - TRAILING_STOP * point
    if new_sl > sl:
        modify_stop_loss(position.ticket, new_sl)
elif position.type == mt5.ORDER_TYPE_SELL:
    new_sl = current_price + TRAILING_STOP * point
    if new_sl < sl:
        modify_stop_loss(position.ticket, new_sl)
```

Definition : Dynamically adjusts the Stop Loss to protect profits from open positions.

Gets all open positions of the symbol.

Calculates a new SL level based on the current price and the Trailing Stop value.

If the new SL is more favorable, call modify_stop_loss.

---

6. modify_stop_loss function

```
def modify_stop_loss(ticket, new_sl):
    request = {
```

```python
"action": mt5.TRADE_ACTION_SLTP,
"position": ticket,
"sl": new_sl,
"tp": None,
}

result = mt5.order_send(request)
if result.retcode != mt5.TRADE_RETCODE_DONE:
    print(f"Error modifying Stop Loss: {result.comment}")
else:
    print(f"Stop Loss updated: {result.order}")
```

Definition : Modifies the Stop Loss of an open position.

Tickets :

ticket: Position identifier.

new_sl: New Stop Loss level.

Sends a request to MetaTrader 5 to modify the SL of the corresponding position.

---

7. Main Loop

```python
try:
    print("Starting the trading script...")
```

```python
while True:
    fast_ma, slow_ma = get_moving_averages(SYMBOL, TIMEFRAME, FAST_PERIOD, SLOW_PERIOD)
    if fast_ma is None or slow_ma is None:
        print("Waiting for sufficient data...")
        time.sleep(10)
        continue

    positions = mt5.positions_total()

    if fast_ma > slow_ma:
        if positions == 0:
            open_position(SYMBOL, "buy", LOT_SIZE, STOP_LOSS, TAKE_PROFIT)
    elif fast_ma < slow_ma:
        if positions == 0:
            open_position(SYMBOL, "sell", LOT_SIZE, STOP_LOSS, TAKE_PROFIT)

    manage_trailing_stop()
    time.sleep(10)
except KeyboardInterrupt:
```

print("Script stopped manually.")

finally:

mt5.shutdown()

Definition : Executes trading logic in a continuous cycle.

Actions :

Calculate moving averages.

Determines whether to open a position based on the crossovers.

Manages the Trailing Stop.

Wait 10 seconds between iterations.

Glossary of Key Python Terms

Script : Text file containing Python code to be executed.

Module : File containing functions, classes or variables that can be imported into other scripts.

Package : Collection of modules organized in a directory with an __init__.py file.

Function : Reusable block of code defined with def that performs a specific task.

Class : Template for creating objects, defined with class.

Object : An instance of a class that has properties (attributes) and behaviors (methods).

Library : A set of modules or packages that extend the capabilities of Python (e.g., pandas, numpy).

DataFrame : Pandas two-dimensional data structure for handling and analyzing tabular data.

List : Ordered collection of elements, allowing duplicates (eg, [1, 2, 3]).

Tuple : An ordered, immutable collection of elements (e.g., (1, 2, 3)).

Dictionary : Data structure that stores key-value pairs (e.g., {"key": "value"}).

Loop : Structure that executes a block of code repeatedly (for, while).

Comprehension : A concise way of constructing lists, dictionaries, or sets (eg, [x**2 for x in range(10)]).

Exception Handling : Mechanism to handle errors using try, except, finally.

Decorator : Function that modifies the behavior of another function or method.

Generator : Function that returns an iterator using yield instead of return.

Lambda : Anonymous function defined with the lambda keyword.

Pandas : Library for tabular data analysis and manipulation.

Numpy : Library for mathematical operations and numerical analysis.

Matplotlib : Library for data visualization using graphs.

Flask : Microframework for web application development.

FastAPI : Modern framework for building fast and efficient APIs.

Jupyter Notebook : Interactive environment for writing and running Python code.

Virtual Environment : Isolated environment for installing project-specific dependencies.

Package Manager : Tool for installing libraries and packages (eg, pip).

Iterable : An object that can be traversed (e.g., lists, strings).

Iterator : An object that produces the elements of an iterable one by one.

Type Hinting : System for indicating data types in functions (e.g., def suma(x: int, y: int) -> int).

REPL : Interactive Python environment (Read-Eval-Print Loop).

Asyncio : Library for asynchronous programming in Python.

Here's a list of the platforms you can use Python on, categorized by purpose:

1. Software Development Platforms

Python is widely used in application, script, and software development in general. These platforms are ideal for working on projects ranging from small scripts to full-fledged applications:

PyCharm : Specialized Python IDE, ideal for advanced projects with debugging support and professional tools.

Visual Studio Code (VS Code) : Versatile, very popular code editor with extensions for Python.

Jupyter Notebook: Interactive scripting environment, ideal for data science and machine learning.

Spyder: IDE focused on scientific calculations and data analysis, used in research.

Thonny: Lightweight IDE designed for Python beginners.

2. Platforms for Data Science and Machine Learning

Python is one of the main tools in data analysis, artificial intelligence and machine learning:

TensorFlow: Framework for building and training deep learning models.

PyTorch: Alternative to TensorFlow, widely used in AI research and development.

Scikit-learn: Library for implementing machine learning and data mining algorithms.

Google Colab: Cloud-based environment for running Jupyter notebooks with GPU/TPU support.

Anaconda: Distribution that includes tools such as Jupyter, Spyder, and scientific libraries pre-installed.

---

3. Platforms for Automation and Scripting

Python is an excellent choice for automating repetitive tasks and developing scripts:

AutoIt with Python: Allows you to automate tasks in Windows.

Selenium: Tool for test automation in web applications.

Robot Framework: Framework for automated testing and repetitive tasks.

Apache Airflow: Platform for workflow automation and orchestration.

---

4. Web Development Platforms

With specialized frameworks, Python allows you to build fast and scalable web applications:

Django: Complete framework for building robust and secure web applications.

Flask: Lightweight framework, ideal for small projects or prototypes.

FastAPI: Modern framework for building fast and efficient APIs.

Pyramid: Flexible framework for projects of any size.

Tornado: Ideal for real-time web applications.

---

5. Financial and Trading Platforms

Python is popular in financial analysis, algorithmic trading, and risk management:

MetaTrader 5 (MT5): Integrates Python for trading strategies and data analysis.

QuantConnect: Python-compatible algorithmic trading platform.

Backtrader: Tool for backtesting trading strategies.

Interactive Brokers (IBKR API): API for automating financial operations.

6. Cloud Platforms

Python is widely supported by cloud services, making it easy to scale and deploy applications:

Google Cloud Platform (GCP): Offers tools such as AI Platform and Cloud Functions with support for Python.

Amazon Web Services (AWS): Supports services such as Lambda, SageMaker, and Elastic Beanstalk.

Microsoft Azure: Ideal for deploying AI solutions and web applications with Python.

Heroku: Allows you to deploy Python applications quickly.

DigitalOcean: Platform for hosting web applications or APIs made in Python.

7. Platforms for Hardware and Electronics

Python is also used to interact with embedded devices and systems:

Raspberry Pi: Platform for electronics and home automation projects.

Arduino (with PyFirmata): Control Arduino boards using Python.

MicroPython: Lightweight version of Python for microcontrollers.

CircuitPython: Similar to MicroPython, oriented towards educational projects.

8. Big Data Platforms

To handle large volumes of data, Python offers support for advanced tools:

Apache Spark (PySpark): Distributed processing of big data.

Dask: Lightweight alternative for handling data in parallel.

Hadoop (Pydoop): Integrates Python into the Hadoop ecosystem.

Databricks: Apache Spark-based platform for advanced data analytics.

9. Platforms for Game Development

Python is also used in the development of video games and simulations:

Pygame: Popular library for creating 2D video games.

Godot Engine: Game development engine that supports Python scripting (GDScript).

Blender: 3D modeling software that allows you to use Python for scripting.

---

10. Industrial Automation Platforms

Python is used in industrial process automation and robotics:

OpenCV: Image processing and computer vision.

ROS (Robot Operating System): Operating system for robotics development.

PyPLC: Industrial process control using PLCs.

Python is extremely versatile and compatible with a wide variety of platforms and tools. Depending on your needs (web development, data analysis, automation, etc.), there's a suitable platform that will maximize your work efficiency.

Thank you for choosing this book as part of your training! I wish you success and determination in your trading career.

You can purchase this book at the following Amazon link :

https://www.amazon.es/dp/B0DQH3Y1B5

Tirso Díaz Díaz

www.ingramcontent.com/pod-product-compliance
Lightning Source LLC
Chambersburg PA
CBHW020645220526
45464CB00001B/304